Young Children's Close Relationships

Individual Differences and Development Series

Robert Plomin, *Series Editor*

The purpose of the **Sage Series on Individual Differences and Development** is to provide a forum for a new wave of research that focuses on individual differences in behavioral development.

Editorial Board

Books in This Series

Young Children's Close Relationships

Beyond Attachment

Judy Dunn

Individual Differences and Development Series
VOLUME 4

LEARNING RESOURCES CENTRE

Havering College
of Further and Higher education

SAGE Publications
International Educational and Professional Publisher
Newbury Park   London   New Delhi

For information address:

SAGE Publications, Inc.
2455 Teller Road
Newbury Park, California 91320
E-mail: order@sagepub.com

SAGE Publications Ltd.
6 Bonhill Street
London EC2A 4PU
United Kingdom

SAGE Publications India Pvt. Ltd.
M-32 Market
Greater Kailash I
New Delhi 110 048 India

Printed in the United States of America

Library of Congress Cataloging-in-Publication Data

Dunn, Judy, 1939-
    Young children's close relationships: beyond attachment / Judy Dunn.
        p.   cm. — (Sage series on individual differences and development; vol. 4)
    Includes bibliographical references and index.
    ISBN 0-8039-4490-X. — ISBN 0-8039-4491-8 (pbk.)
    1. Mother and child. 2. Brothers and sisters. 3. Friendship in children. 4. Individual differences in children. 5. Interpersonal relations in children. I. Title. II. Series.
BF723.M55D86   1993
155.4'18—dc20
                                                                    93-6871
                                                                    CIP

00   01   02   03   10 9 8 7 6 5

Sage Production Editor: Judith L. Hunter

Contents

Figures

Preface

The impetus for this book came from the experience of watching and listening to young children in the context of three of their close relationships—with mother, sibling, and close friend—and from talking to them about these relationships. The complexity of each relationship and the individual differences in each were striking. Studying young children with their mothers, siblings, and friends reveals not only the differences in the security of their attachment to their mothers but also the range of other dimensions in which these relationships differ. And, I shall argue, these differences raise serious questions about current perspectives on individual differences in children's close relationships and their origins.

We widely accept that the quality of parent-child (and chiefly mother-child) relationships influences children's future relationships, and the key dimension of that all-important mother-child relationship is seen as *security of attachment*. Yet the relationships we have studied appear so complex, rich, and varied—and the differences between children so marked—that surely these differences, and the subtlety and variety of these early relationships, deserve attention. And certainly the nature of the links between the mother-child relationship and these very different relationships that children form with other children merits careful examination.

This book examines those differences in relationships as well as the connections among them. Each relationship is first described in terms of the dimensions that appear, on theoretical grounds, to be good candidates for developmental influence. Then we turn to the key issue of the links between children's relationships with mothers, with siblings, and with friends. I will draw on a range of current studies, especially three ongoing research projects: the Pennsylvania Sibling Study (Dunn, Brown, Slomkowski, Tesla, & Youngblade, 1991), the Cambridge Sibling Study (Dunn, Brown, & Beardsall, 1991; Dunn & Munn, 1987), and the Colorado Sibling Study (Stocker, Dunn, & Plomin, 1989). The first of these projects is supported by a grant from NICHD (HD-23158), the second by the Medical Research Council of Great Britain and a grant from NIMH (MH-46535), and the third by a grant from NSF (BNS-8806589). In each project we have studied children over several years from the preschool period, as they grow up with their mothers and siblings, and also with their friends. I am extremely grateful for the constructive criticism of this book given by Michael Rutter and Robert Hinde.

We begin with some general questions: Why are individual differences in relationships in childhood seen as important? How can we set about describing them?

Individual Differences in Relationships

Young children differ notably in their relationships with their parents: Even siblings within the same family can have strikingly different relationships with the same mother and father. Children also differ in their relationships with their siblings, which can include close intimacy or indifference, loving affection or disparagement and hostility.

Marked and poignant differences are evident as well in the number and the nature of friendships that children enjoy. One child is happily a member of a circle of companions, another has just one intense and close friendship, another is without friends. What do we know of the origins of these differences in children's close relationships? Are they linked to one another? Does a troubled parent-child relationship imply that a child will have difficulties in making friends in later life?

The idea that differences in children's relationships with their parents are centrally important in their development is key in the grand theories of psychological development (e.g., Erikson, 1950; Freud, 1949). And the belief that a child's relationship with his or her mother profoundly affects the quality of relationships formed later in life has wide currency today: The parent-child relationship is seen as a crucial influence on the construction of later close relationships by many clinicians and developmental psychologists. Interest in young children's relationships, however, is broadening now from a previously exclusive focus on parents and children. Recent years have seen a burst of empirical research on children's relationships not only with their parents but also with their siblings, friends, and peer groups—and on the links between and among these different relationships. This book is concerned with the nature, development, and implications of individual differences in these relationships in early childhood and with the links between these different relationships. The focus on individual differences in relationships is especially relevant now, given the new acknowledgement by developmental psychologists of the extent to which relationships may be important in development.

Relationships and Development

For children's social and emotional development, the significance of early close relationships has long been assumed (Bowlby, 1982; Freud, 1949). Relationships are viewed as the contexts in which socialization takes place (Hartup, 1986; Maccoby & Martin, 1983), in which communication skills are acquired, in which the regulation of emotions develops (Garber & Dodge, 1991), and in which the self system has its origins (Berscheid, 1986; Harter, 1983; Sullivan, 1953). A secure relationship between child and mother is seen as not only the basis for a child's sense of self-efficacy and social skills, but also of key significance in the development of later close relationships (Bretherton & Waters, 1985; Mahler, Pine, & Bergman, 1975; Sroufe & Fleeson, 1986).

More recently, theorists also have been increasingly interested in the links between relationships and cognitive development. Cognitive development was formerly conceptualized chiefly in terms of an individual actively exploring and acting on his or her environment in an autonomous fashion. Now, however, the social interactions and relationships within which children grow up are widely accepted as important in their cognitive development, both in fundamental cognitive advances and influencing cognitive performance.

The interest of researchers in the connections between cognitive advance and social interaction shows up in widely differing domains and theoretical approaches. Those who are interested in cognitive development in early infancy, for instance, argue convincingly that the social exchanges in which babies engage play a part in their growing understanding (Bryant, 1985). Babies are born endowed to interact with others, and their principal "tools" for achieving their ends are other human beings (Bruner, 1983). It is also evident that the acquisition of language—with all that this implies for the development of understanding and membership of a cultural world—takes place in the context of social relationships, and that individual differences in language acquisition are affected by early social experiences. Within a different framework, the ideas of Vygotsky (1978)—which hold that cognitive advances are set firmly in the context of social interaction—are receiving increasing attention and empirical support (Rogoff, 1990). And a flourishing line of research currently is examining the ways in which exposure to the different perspective of another person influences cognitive development (e.g., Damon & Phelps, 1989; Doise & Mugny, 1984; Foot, Morgan, & Shute, 1990). The chief emphasis in this work on cognitive development and social interaction has been on normative development, but the ideas and findings clearly raise important questions about how differences in such social experiences may affect children's cognitive development.

More generally, it is clear that perception and classification of experience are profoundly affected by the cultural world in which individuals grow up, and such cultural influences are mediated chiefly through differences in relationships (Hinde, 1987): We increasingly see that a "'relationships' approach is crucial for many issues in the social sciences, including the understanding of how individuals affect and are affected by the society in which they live" (Hinde, 1987, p. vii). Hinde (1979, 1987) has argued that we must appreciate the connections between the quality of relationships and both the wider social context and, at the other extreme, differences in individuals. The argument has gained a sympathetic audience. We must recognize, he emphasizes, the distinction between different levels of social complexity: from individual behavior to interactions, to relationships, to group and sociocultural structure. We also have to examine the relations between these different levels of social processes, the connections between them, as shown in Figure 1.1. We must further acknowledge that relations between relationships are two-way, each affecting the other, and that norms within families are not just superimposed but created by interactions and relationships between family members. The importance of our efforts to describe and understand these connections is gaining wide recognition.

And from yet another perspective—the interest of geneticists in the development of individual differences in personality and psychopathology—we see new attention on the different relationships that are experienced by siblings growing up within the same family. The behavioral genetic research has shown that the salient environmental influences that affect individual development work within, rather than between, families: To explain individual differences in development, we must explain why children within the same family are so different from one another. Their different relationships are clearly one important source of such "nonshared" experiences. There is now increasing interest in documenting how such differences in relationships are linked to individual outcome (Dunn & Plomin, 1990).

Thus, for a wide spectrum of developmental concerns—ranging from the question of when and why children make cognitive advances to the issue of how cultural institutions affect individual development—the importance of a deeper understanding of the nature and development of differences in relationships is becoming clear. To understand the significance of such differences, we need an adequate description of the key dimensions in which the relationships differ. How can we set about describing such differences?

Describing Relationships

Compare the relationships of three 4-year-olds (Amy, Tina, and Nat) with their respective mothers, all of whom participated in a study of families in Pennsylvania (Dunn, Brown, Slomkowski,

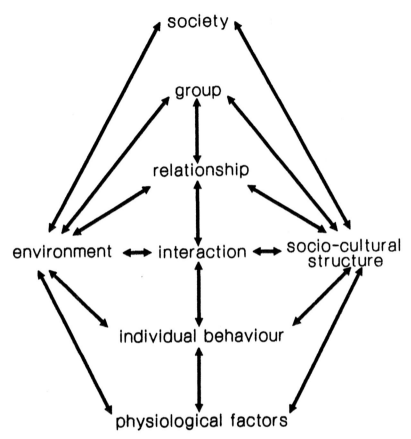

Figure 1.1. The Relations Between Successive Levels of Social Complexity (from Hinde, 1992; copyright 1992 by the American Psychological Association).

Tesla, & Youngblade, 1991). Amy's parents are hard-working farmers living in an old house in the country; her mother spends long hours working in the barn next to the house, and Amy and her older brother are often left in charge of their two younger siblings—a pattern quite common among rural farming families. Amy goes to her mother when she is hurt, wants something to eat, or is in need of help, but not usually for entertainment or conversation. Most of her time at home is spent playing with her siblings. Her mother is always busy with farm work or housework and expects all her children to obey her promptly, which they do. We observe few extended arguments between parents and children in this family. Amy is an independent, resilient child, initially shy with unfamiliar people but then friendly and talkative.

In contrast to the apparently detached relationship between Amy and her mother, consider Tina, who lives in a housing development on the edge of the nearby town. Tina's mother delights in her three daughters, and we see a running stream of joking, chatting, and storytelling between them all as they do things together. Then consider Nat, who is like Amy, a child growing up in a rural family with two parents who work all day. In contrast to Amy, however, Nat spends the time that his parents are around pretty close to them; they share his interest and pleasure in particular television programs and are amused by his jokes and discoveries. Much of the time he is around his father as he works in the basement; their exchanges have a calm, affectionate tenor.

A visitor to these three families would be struck by the differences between the three mother-child pairs. Tina, an expressive and emotional child, is always on and off her mother's knee, laughing with her and arguing with her. She often refuses to do what she's asked: "She gets her way round all of us—she has an answer for everything!" her mother comments ruefully. Nat is also an expressive child, but everything is lower in key. He wanders off to pick flowers for his mother—but, as his mother notes, "He doesn't go in for cuddles." Conflicts with his parents are only occasional and are quiet in tone. What do the differences in these relationships—obvious at an anecdotal level—imply for the children's future development? How can we move from such an impressionistic image of the differences to a more systematic description of relationships, one that would allow us to investigate the developmental importance—if any—of the differences among them?

Even such an anecdotal account illustrates some key issues that must be considered when we think about relationships. At the outset we have to recognize that progress in describing and understanding individual differences in relationships requires us to deal with a range of influences that are of very different kinds. This brings us back to that argument set out by Hinde, that we must recognize the links between the qualities of relationships and both the wider cultural context and the contribution of the individuals involved. As Figure 1.1 implies, we must consider several different levels of description and influence: the level of the individual and the characteristics he or she brings to the relationship (Tina's lively, outgoing, and emotional personality, for instance); the level of the interactions between the two in the relationship (the jokes, arguments, and conversations Tina has with her mother); the level of the relationship, which takes into account the patterns of interaction over a long time span, shared expectations, and the balance of their relative contributions to the relationship. And, finally, there is the level of the social world beyond the dyad—the impact of other family relationships, the norms and expectations concerning relationships held in that particular cultural group, and the influence of social networks and social institutions on the relationships within the family.

One important idea in this framework as set out by Hinde is that each level has properties that are different from those of the other levels. For instance, we might focus on the close involvement between Tina and her mother. This idea of *involvement* necessarily includes two or more people; so "involvement" is a dimension that is appropriate at the level of interaction or relationship rather than at the level of an individual. We might also focus on how well Tina and her mother *mesh* in their responses to one another, and so "meshing" is a descriptive idea that involves more than one person and is relevant to the level of interaction or relationship. (However, to complicate matters, we should note that Tina may be an individual who tends to "mesh" easily in a wide range of other relationships, and thus we could also think of a "propensity to mesh" as an individual's characteristic.) And if we focused on Tina's relationships with her older sister, Katy, we would note the *complementary* nature of their relationship, with Katy the organizing, caretaking, and supportive older sister, and Tina the compliant, dependent partner. The quality of "complementariness" is relevant to the relationship level, not to that of the individual. And the particular adjustment of Tina and her mother to each other means that some features of their relationship are special and are not evident in the relationships that each has with other people. As Ross and Lollis (1989) note in their discussion of Kenny's social relations model (Kenny & La Voie, 1984), which distinguishes influences of individuals from those of the relationship between them:

> The relationship itself can have an impact that goes beyond the characteristic influences of either member: in the social relations model, relationship effects reflect the special adjustment of an actor to a particular partner. When two people bring out qualities in one another that are neither exhibited nor elicited in their other relationships, then their behavior cannot be predicted based on knowledge of actor and partner effects.

A second general point is that each level in the model shown in Figure 1.1 is affected by other levels. How Tina and her mother interact is affected not only by both of their personalities (individual level), but also by their shared history and expectations of joint pleasures (relationship level). Indeed, Hinde has emphasized that no aspect of what an individual does in interaction with another is independent of the shared history of their relationship. How they relate is also influenced by the wider world in which they live—the level of the cultural world outside the family. Tina's mother holds strong views on how mothers and children should get along and on what is reasonable to expect of her 4-year-old daughter, and these ideas are shared by many in her cultural world. A moment's reflection on Amy and Tina shows the relevance of the cultural context to differences in their relationships. In Tina's world, expressing oneself and providing reasons for a point of view are valued aspects of children's behavior, and children are encouraged to assert themselves in these ways. The idea that parents should be responsive to their children's needs and demands is also widely held, and even as a toddler Tina expected to have her requests taken seriously.

In contrast, for the families in Amy's world, children are expected to take on responsibilities and to be independent, and they are not to expect their parents to drop everything and attend to their every whim. They are expected to be obedient, and the patterns of control between parent and child are very different from those in many families in Tina's world. Every relationship is set within a particular cultural context, and different cultural expectations color and influence the course of the development of the relationship between parents and children.

For the psychologist, recognizing these differences is an important step. It means that we have to be sure our measures and descriptive tools are not based on the assumption that what is "normal" or best is chiefly what our own cultural world views as optimal for children. The contrast between what is expected of Amy and of Tina alerts us to the importance of expectations and of norms within the family and in the social world beyond.

But a focus on such cultural differences alone does not take us very far in the exploration of individual differences. Nat comes from the same rural community as Amy, yet his relationship with his mother and father is very different from hers. Even within the same family, fathers and mothers can have very different relationships with the same child, and parent-child relationships can be strikingly different with the various children in the family, as we will discuss in Chapter 5. The usefulness of the model in Figure 1.1 lies in the way it draws our attention to the necessity of moving between these different levels if we are to understand fully any individual differences in relationships. For example, in his work on rhesus monkey babies and their mothers, Hinde showed that understanding individual differences in how baby monkeys react to short separations from their mothers requires studying the relationship between the baby and mother as well as how that relationship was affected by the group setting in which the mother-baby pair lived (Hinde, 1979).

The principles Hinde set out from studying these monkey families and from his own work with children are strikingly relevant for understanding differences in children's relationships. He made clear that the course of an interaction between a child and her parent, friend, or sibling is dependent both on the "natures of the participating individuals and on the relationship of which it forms part, and the nature of the relationship is influenced both by the component interactions, and by the group in which it is embedded" (Hinde, in press).

So this is the framework within which we will look at those striking differences in young children's relationships, one in which the key links are between the quality of relationships and individual differences in children and their partners on the one hand and the wider social context on the other.

Relationships and Social Understanding

An important starting point for our exploration of differences in early relationships is the new appreciation of very young children's social awareness and understanding, an appreciation that has developed from both recent work on children within their families and experimental studies. From a range of different lines of research we have gained a new picture of what children understand about themselves and other people, as well as information on the extent of their interest in and sensitivity to other people. We have learned also that, from their second year, children are increasingly articulate participants in discussion of their own relationships, those of others, and more generally of the rules and expectations within their own social worlds (Dunn, 1988a). A central argument in this work is that this new view of children's social understanding has major implications for the nature and development of individual differences in their relationships, implications that will be examined in three themes that run through the book: (1) influences on children's relationships other than the direct interaction between parent and child; (2) the significance of communication, perception, and cognition in children's relationships; and (3) the contribution of differences in children's individual characteristics.

BEYOND THE PARENT-CHILD DYAD

The first theme is that the salient socioemotional influences on children's developing relationships extend well beyond the direct interaction between children and their parents, which was the major and often the exclusive focus of research until quite recently. For example, children are highly responsive to emotional interaction between others and to the quality of other relationships within the family, such as the marital relationship or the relationship between their siblings and their parents. This sensitivity to emotional exchanges between other family members has been demonstrated, for instance, in a classic series of studies by Zahn-Waxler and her colleagues (Zahn-Waxler & Radke-Yarrow, 1982), in research on children's reactions to interaction between their mothers and siblings (Dunn & Munn, 1985), and in experimental studies in which children witness angry exchanges between others (Cummings, 1987). Such experiences have clear effects, both immediate and over time, on children's play and interaction with peers.

COMMUNICATION, PERCEPTION, AND COGNITION

The second theme arising from the recent research on social understanding concerns the significance of language and communication, perception, and cognition in children's relationships. In the study of adult relationships, the importance of communication, especially *verbal* communication, and of understanding the goals, beliefs, and desires of others are rightly given major prominence. It is argued not only that self-disclosure is a prerequisite for satisfactory relationship development (e.g., Miell & Duck, 1986) but also and much more broadly that "individuals communicate and maintain, develop, or diminish their relationship by the symbolic uses that they make of language and the general forms of communicative structure that they employ. . . . Uses of language . . . are at some level what the relationship is" (Duck, 1989, pp. 98-100). Perceptions and memories are also seen as key in adult relationships. To quote Duck again, "The ways . . . in which relational events are remembered are obviously a critical factor in the competent development of relationships, their maintenance, and perhaps their breakdown or disruption—in children as well as in adults" (Duck, 1989, p. 102).

But is such a focus on language and understanding appropriate or relevant for relationships in early childhood? After all, this is a period when the major focus of those who study relationships has been on the nonverbal expression of emotional security of attachment between children and their mothers. This book argues that what we now know of children's social understanding makes a focus on language and understanding essential not only for a full description of children's relationships, but also for progress in understanding individual differences in their development. Children from their second year onward talk about feelings—their own and those of other people (Brown & Dunn, 1991). They inquire about and debate why people behave the way they do (Dunn & Brown, 1992). And over the preschool years, they develop an increasingly firm grasp of the links between people's behavior and their intentions, desires, and beliefs (Astington, Harris, & Olson, 1989; Wellman, 1990). Just as the work on children's sensitivity to emotional interaction between others carries the message that salient influences on individual differences extend beyond the parent-child dyad, so too a focus on children's talk highlights the fact that even preschool children are family members and members of a culture beyond their own immediate family. By the age of 3, they refer to social rules and expectations that are the currency of the wider social world, and indeed their relationships with their parents and siblings differ in different cultures (Bornstein, 1991; Zukow, 1989).

The implications of this sophistication in social understanding for their relationships are several. First, children use their understanding of what is expected and appropriate behavior in their intimate relationships in a range of different ways: to excuse themselves, blame others, intervene or disrupt others' interactions, and to support or comfort others (Dunn, 1988a). They also use their knowledge of others' emotions—that is, their grasp of what will annoy, amuse, interest, or console those who share their family world. The nature of their relationships is intimately linked to their cognitive sophistication, and any attempt to understand individual differences in those relationships must account for the significance of relative differences in this sophistication.

Second, children begin to engage in conversations about themselves and other people from their second year onward, and evaluative talk about self and others forms one strand in their close relationships from early in the preschool period. Processes of influence on the development of their relationships, then, operate not only at a broad emotional level, such as the dimensions of "emotional responsiveness" that are deemed to be important in the development of security of attachment, but also at levels involving cognitive processes. Thus, as we will see, differences in family discourse involving attributional and evaluative "messages" are found to be systematically related to differences in the quality of children's later relationships.

Does this emphasis on the links between children's relationships and their communication and social understanding imply that we should equate differences in the quality of those relationships with some set of skills or cognitive competencies? The answer offered here is an emphatic *no*. The new view of children's social understanding enormously enriches our view of the nature of early relationships, but we would, paradoxically, make a major mistake if we attributed differences in the quality of those relationships simply to differences in social or cognitive competence. A key argument of this book is that this social understanding can be used in very different ways within relationships. It can be employed to resolve conflict, to increase harmony, support, comfort, or amuse the other—or it can be used to provoke, dominate, subdue, tease, and denigrate. The key to capturing individual differences in children's relationships is to describe not only the extent of social understanding revealed but also how it is used in the relationship.

And from the research that focuses on the same children in a range of their different relationships we have powerful evidence against the idea that differences in relationships can be attributed simply to differences in cognitive competencies. The various relationships that children form—with fathers, mothers, siblings, and friends—are markedly different in the demands and rewards they present. Even within the general category of *friendships*, for example, different kinds of relationships are included, and these present very different challenges to children's sociocognitive sophistication. As we will see, the same child can display very different social "competence" in different relationships. He or she may be adept at resolving conflict through negotiation and conciliation in one relationship but behave quite differently in another relationship with no such sophisticated attempts at resolution. This book will argue that we should move away from a simple notion of the "competent" or "incompetent" child and toward a differentiated view of relationships in early childhood. Sociocognitive capacities are used differently in different relationships, even by the same individual, depending on the quality of those relationships. Furthermore, I will suggest that such differences in relationships in turn foster the development of individual differences in social understanding.

INDIVIDUAL DIFFERENCES IN CHILDREN

The third general theme running through these discussions of children's different relationships concerns the significance of the role of individual differences in children's personalities and characteristics. The discussions will underline the importance of acknowledging the key contribution of differences in children's temperament, humor, argumentativeness, self-confidence, and intellectual curiosity to differences in their various relationships. The connections between such individual characteristics and the qualities of relationships are likely to be two-way: For example, children's experiences within their relationships will influence in turn their own qualities of humor and self-confidence.

These three themes—first, that salient socioemotional influences on children's developing relationships extend well beyond the direct interaction of parent and child; second, that children's social understanding, perceptions, and communications concerning self and other are important from early in childhood; and third, that individual differences in children's characteristics make major contributions to their relationships—will be examined in the context of children's relationships with their parents, their siblings, and their friends. For each set of relationships considered, the following general questions concerning relationships will be discussed: What are the dimensions on which children's relationships differ? What are the origins of these differences? What are the implications of such differences for children's development?

We begin with the relationships of children and their parents.

Parents and Children

Two approaches to describing differences in the relationships of parents and children have dominated psychologists' writing and research. The first has emphasized parenting and the socialization of children; this approach has a very extensive literature. Second, a wealth of research has focused on attachments between young children and their parents.

Research on Parenting

Research into socialization and parenting is focused primarily on what parents do with their children rather than on the dyadic relationship. For instance, in the case of Amy, Tina, and Nat (described in Chapter 1), studies in this framework would describe the differences in parental acceptance or responsiveness shown by their mothers and in the extent and style of control and discipline the mothers try to exercise. One of the most influential descriptive schemes here is that of Baumrind (1971); it distinguishes four different styles of parenting based on the two dimensions of acceptance-rejection and controlling-permissiveness. *Authoritative* parents are demanding and accepting, *authoritarian* parents are demanding and rejecting, *permissive* parents are permissive and accepting, and *neglecting* parents are permissive and ignoring or rejecting. The significance of differences in parents' behavior along these dimensions has been explored in many studies and related to a variety of outcomes, such as moral development, perceived self-competence, and aggression (reviewed in Maccoby and Martin, 1983).

We must recognize, however, that such differences in "parenting" may very well be closely linked both to differences in children and the previous history of interaction between child and parent. Recall that important principle stressed by Hinde: No measure of either individual in an interaction is independent of the previous history of interactions between them. In commonsensical terms, feeling warm about and showing affection to a child who is typically expressive, outgoing, and affectionate to you is easier than with a moody, contrary child. Flexibility and patience are easier in controlling a child who has always complied easily and cheerfully than with a child who is frequently contrary, complaining, and stubborn.

Studies of families with more than one child show that the same parents feel and behave rather differently toward individual children in terms of both warmth and discipline or control (Dunn & Plomin, 1990). Differences in how children behave are closely implicated in the dimensions of "parental" behavior outlined in the Baumrind model. And the study of "parenting" per se will not take us very far in understanding the development of individual differences in parent-child relationships unless it also focuses on the contribution of both parents and children to their interaction, on developmental changes in the dimensions described, and on how these dimensions are affected by influences in the social world beyond the parent-child dyad.

Also note that the great majority of studies of parenting are studies of mothers' behavior. We are still strikingly ignorant about many aspects of fathers' behavior and relationships (Harris & Morgan, 1991). This gap in research on fathers is just as evident in the second approach to relationships—the study of attachment.

Security of Attachment

The second main approach to studying individual differences in what happens between parents and children focuses more explicitly on the relationship level. Within the framework of attachment theory, our attention is on a typology of differences in a dimension of security in children's relationships with their parents. To appreciate the profound importance of this dimension of security for very young children, one must only watch toddlers playing and exploring an unfamiliar place, such as a doctor's waiting room. While their mothers or fathers are in the room, most young children will begin to wander round the waiting room, investigating the toys and furniture and playing with what they find, checking back occasionally with a glance at their parents. But if a parent leaves the room, the child's behavior is often dramatically transformed. The happy, confident explorer becomes distraught, distressed—unable to play or calm down without some comforting intervention. As attachment theorists have shown, parents provide a "secure base" from which children can explore with confidence. Watch a young child when an unfamiliar person arrives in her home: How the child reacts will differ greatly, depending on whether a parent or sibling is present. The child may exhibit a happy, interested, sociable curiosity about the stranger when her parent or older sibling is around; the same child often panics if the parent leaves the room to make a cup of coffee. The toddler may well scramble to get close to a parent or sibling in the stranger's presence.

These signals of distress—and the attempts to get close to a parent when separated or when faced with a novel or fear-inducing situation—are seen in Bowlby's (1969, 1973) attachment theory to be actions that have key biological and developmental functions. From his original concern as a clinician with the effects on children of institutional experiences or disrupted mothering, Bowlby developed a far-reaching theory on the developmental significance of early social relationships; in this theory he applied an evolutionary perspective to his clinical ideas, drawing from ethological work on the tie between mother and infant in nonhuman primates.

Within this theoretical approach, children's distress at separation and their attempts to renew closeness with their mothers are seen as part of a system that brings mother and child close together at moments of danger, a system that may have functioned to protect the young from predators in the environment in which humans first evolved.

Bowlby proposed that, from the interaction that this system ensured, an attachment relationship between child and caregiver developed, and the relative security or insecurity of this relationship influenced the child's later emotional relationships and personality: "[A]n unthinking confidence in the unfailing accessibility and support of attachment figures is the bedrock on which stable and self-reliant personality is built" (Bowlby, 1973, p. 322). Bowlby's theory cannot be described with justice in the limited space here; for recent summaries and discussion, see Bowlby (1988), Ainsworth and Bowlby (1991), and Rutter (1991). The three key themes of his theory, however, are (1) an emphasis on the security dimension, as differentiated from other aspects of the relationship; (2) a stress on selective attachments as key to security and later optimal socioemotional development; and (3) the idea that later close relationships are built on the basis of the first attachment relationship. Our present focus is on the differences in children's security in their relationship with their parents and on the question of what inferences we can make about security as a property of their relationships from the conventional approach psychologists use—that is, by measuring children's response to separation and reunion with their parents.

Bowlby's theory was originally concerned with the course of normative socioemotional and personality development in children. Ideas on the development, antecedents, and consequences of individual differences in security of attachment have grown chiefly from the pioneering work of Mary Ainsworth (Ainsworth & Bowlby, 1991). Very large differences are clearly seen in the extent to which children are upset by their mother's departure and in the intensity with which they demand her attention and enjoy her presence. Clearly, too, children express their attachment to their mothers in different ways. Some like to stay close but do not want to be held, some want a lot of cuddling, and some are happy when wandering away but like to have a lot of "conversation" and attention from their parents. The balance between exploring the world and maintaining safe contact is maintained in a rich and subtle variety of ways by different parent-child pairs, a range of communication and understanding that varies greatly in intensity and expression. How much any individual child will request these different kinds of contact will also vary with how he or she is feeling (the degree to which she is tired or frustrated, for example), with the particular situation (how novel or familiar it is), and with developmental stage.

But as Ainsworth has pointed out, this variation in any individual child's behavior does not mean that the underlying relationship is unstable. She argues that we need to distinguish between the expression of attachment and the underlying relationship bond. Wanting to be near the mother may be only one of the things a child wants. He may also want to explore and play away from his mother. But whereas this distinction between the expression of attachment and the underlying relationship is important, it leaves us with a real problem. If the expression of attachment varies even within the same child, despite the stability of the bond itself, how can we identify differences between child-parent pairs in the underlying bond?

The strategy that Ainsworth developed, and which has proved extraordinarily fruitful, was to examine differences in children's response to a standardized series of separations and reunions with their mothers in a laboratory setting—the *Strange Situation* (Ainsworth & Wittig, 1969). From an examination of the individual differences in children's responses to these potentially stressful episodes of separation from and reunion with their parents, a typology of differences in the security of the relationship has been developed in which distinctions are made between children whose relationships with their mothers are seen as *secure, insecure-avoidant, insecure-ambivalent/resistant*, or *insecure-disorganized*. Children are considered to be securely attached if they show distress at their parents' absence but greet them positively when they return and are able to use them as a base from which to explore. Those who are not distressed at their parents' departure and ignore their return are seen as insecure-avoidant, while those who are highly distressed by the parents' departure and fail to settle or explore on reunion are categorized as insecure-resistant/ambivalent. The fourth category, insecure-disorganized, was developed after studies of clinical samples showed that some children could not be categorized in the first three groups.

A huge body of research literature now maps the antecedents and later correlates of individual differences in these categories of children's attachment to their mothers (Belsky & Nezworski, 1988; Bretherton & Waters, 1985; Sroufe, 1983), research to which we will return when we consider the links between children's relationships with parents, siblings, and peers (Chapter 6). It is a literature that has provided clear theoretical predictions and a mass of useful empirical findings, many of which support the main tenets of the theory, such as evidence for links between differences in the extent of maternal sensitivity and responsiveness shown in early mother-child interaction and later security of attachment shown in Strange Situation behavior (Belsky & Cassidy, in press, will provide a review). However, within this framework of attachment, several key issues concerning relationships remain unexplored.

Dimensions of Difference

First, consider the importance of aspects of the relationship between parent and child other than the dimension of security. Clearly, security is a feature of young children's relationships that is of major importance, and it is one that continues to be important as children grow up, though it is expressed differently. But think of the relationships that Tina, Amy, and Nat have with their parents. These differ in several other dimensions that might well appear likely to be important for the children's development. For example, they differ in dimensions of a broad emotional nature: in mutual warmth, the frequency with which mother and child enjoy moments of expressed affection, and in the frequency of conflict. They differ in shared involvement in daily activities. They also differ in dimensions that include both emotional and cognitive aspects, such as shared communication about feelings, shared humor (a key feature of adult intimate relationships), and self-disclosure. They differ also in the pattern of power and control in the relationship—not just parental control, but also control by children. All of these features are considered important in adult relationships; might they not also be important in the relationships between young children and their parents?

The early research on attachment relationships showed us that different dimensions of the relationship between child and parent were affected differently by stressful circumstances. For example, research revealed that playful interactions decreased when children were under stress, while approaches to the attachment figure increased. This was a particularly useful lesson from the attachment research; ironically, however, partly as a result of the domination of attachment theory in the study of developing relationships, most research into parent-child relationships has not looked beyond the dimension of attachment security to other aspects of these relationships. [Notable exceptions here are the studies of the Grossmans, which demonstrate the independence of the qualities of parents as playmates, teachers, and caregivers (Grossman & Grossman, 1991), and that of Hinde (1982).] When the framework is broadened, the results show that these other dimensions are indeed important. For example, consider the idea that differences in mutual involvement of parent and child may be important. In a recent longitudinal study of families with children in middle childhood, McHale, Crouter, and their colleagues assessed differences in mutual involvement that included measures of how much time the parent and child spent together, what they were doing together (for instance, whether they were working together or playing), and what the social context of their activities was. The results showed that differences in parent-child involvement were orthogonal to other aspects of the relationship, such as parents' and children's perceptions of the warmth of the relationship; when differences in involvement were juxtaposed with other dimensions, there were powerful correlations with aspects of child outcome, such as children's sense of their own competence and self-worth. What provided the predictive power was involvement combined with mutual warmth (McHale, Crouter, & Bartko, in press).

What about more cognitive aspects of the relationship? Those who study adult relationships put shared intimacy and self-disclosure high on the list of important dimensions. Yet intimacy, sharing feelings, and self-disclosure are hardly mentioned by those who study early parent-child relationships (see, however, Hinde, 1987). Are such features of relationships inappropriate before children reach adolescence? The recent work on social understanding alerts us to the importance of recognizing that children are thinking members of their families even during preschool years (Dunn, 1988a; Wellman, 1990). Let's take just three dimensions of relationships that have received attention in research on adults, which the new perspective on young children's social understanding suggests may be important even in early childhood.

First, sharing feelings and experiences with another is an aspect of intimacy that is thought to be important in adolescent and adult relationships. Even as preschoolers, some children show considerable curiosity about their parents' feelings, intentions, and worries, although in such curiosity are marked individual differences. Consider the following examples, drawn from our observational studies of children and their parents. The first, from an observation of a Cambridge mother with her secondborn son, illustrates children's curiosity about what their mothers are feeling.

The mother has been telling an observer about how she had been frightened by discovering a dead mouse behind a chair. The child eagerly interrupted the conversation between his mother and the observer.

C: What's that frighten you, Mum?
M: Nothing.
C: What's that frighten you?
M: Nothing.
C: What is it? . . . What's that down there, Mummy? That frighten you.
M: Nothing!
C: That not frighten you?
M: No. Didn't frighten me.

What's striking is that the child was only 28 months old. His concern and interest in his mother's feelings, however, are clear. The next example, from an observation of Tina, who was first mentioned in Chapter 1, illustrates her mother's characteristic style of talking to her children about her own experiences.

Tina's mother tells her children, who are turning somersaults, about a nightmare she had the previous night.

> *M:* Oh, I wanted to tell you a dream I had last night! . . . Oh my word, it was a nightmare!
> *Sibling:* What?
> *M:* I dreamed I did that [a back somersault] and for some reason I lost my breath or something. And I was so afraid and I was shouting "Help me! Help me!" And I must have woke up. And it was a nightmare—I couldn't get out of it and I couldn't breathe! I shouted "Help me! Help me!" It scares me even to think about it. It was the weirdest dream!

Tina and her sister listened, riveted to their mother's account, and then Tina's sister started talking about her dream.

This Pennsylvania study was notable for the range of individual differences between mother-child pairs in the frequency and extent of such conversations about feelings—both others' and their own. A similar range of individual differences was found in a sample of families in England (Dunn, Brown, & Beardsall, 1991) in which the differences ranged from mother-child pairs who discussed feelings in more than 30 speaker turns per hour to pairs who never talked about feelings during our observations.

Shared humor is a second dimension that is clearly important in adult relationships. Its significance lies both in the shared warm emotions enjoyed together and in the intimacy that is reflected when two individuals each know what the other will find funny. However, this dimension has been almost completely ignored in studies of parent-child relationships, where the emphasis has been chiefly on the grimmer features of insecurity, insensitivity, lack of responsiveness, and so on. Yet any observer of families with young children cannot fail to be impressed by the jokes and humor that many parents and children share—the delight they have in finding things funny together. These jokes begin extremely early: during the first year of life when babies begin to find the antics of their parents and siblings uproariously funny (Sroufe & Wunsch, 1972). In the early months of the second year, it is not just simple clowning and slapstick by parents that is a source of shared laughter, but the children themselves are often the clowns, as the next two examples, drawn from observations of 18-month-old toddlers, illustrate:

> Child puts potty on head, looks at mother and at observer, and smiles.

> Child sits on potty fully clothed (not asked to do so), looks at mother. Child grunts heavily and says "Poo!" Grunts heavily again: "Poo! Poo!" Gets up, looks at Mother, picks up empty potty and waves it at mother, laughing.

The differences between mother-child pairs in the frequency with which they joke together are very marked. For instance, among the families who participated in one of our Cambridge studies, the frequency of shared jokes between mothers and their 36-month-old children ranged from none to 16 in an hour, and in our Pennsylvanian study the range was equally great (McGhee, 1989).

Connectedness is a third dimension that has received much attention in studies of adolescents' family relationships, as well as in research on children's friendships (Cooper, Grotevant, & Condon, 1983; Gottman, 1986). We define it as the degree to which two individuals sustain a connected thread of communication when they interact. In research on children's friendship, for example, studies of the degree of connectedness in the conversation between pairs of children who were just becoming acquainted led to powerful predictions of which dyads of children would become close friends over time (Parker, 1986). Yet connectedness has not often been considered as a dimension of young children's relationships with their parents, even though differences between mother-child pairs in the connectedness of their communication are marked. Amy and her mother, for instance, typically had extremely brief exchanges (an average of two conversational turns), whereas Tina and her mother engaged in long conversations in which both partners were "tuned in" to each other's contribution.

Each of these aspects of the relationships between parents and children—self-disclosure and discourse about feelings, shared humor, and connectedness—is deemed important in the relationships of older individuals. Each shows a wide range of differences in families with young children, and each can be reliably measured, even with preschool-aged children. We are still ignorant, however, about how each dimension relates to other aspects of parent-child relationships. Is shared humor highly correlated with shared warmth assessed in other ways? Are connectedness, talk about feelings, and humor in fact all closely related? In examining them, are we simply picking up on some broad dimension of differences in positive parent-child relationships? To what extent would examining each aspect of the relationship separately give us purchase on different outcome measures of children's development or relationships? How far is each correlated with security of attachment?

These matters are only just beginning to be examined, but already we see hints that it is useful to delineate these different features of parent-child relationships and their separate, independent associations with children's outcome. For example, consider the differences in parent-child joint discussion of feelings and in self-disclosure. Considerable interest has recently been shown in the family correlates and antecedents of children's understanding of others' feelings, because children differ markedly in this core aspect of human development (Denham, 1986). What lies behind such differences in understanding?

Several proposals have been made concerning the family experiences that may contribute to them. Differences in attachment security, parental emotional expressiveness, and parental involvement and responsiveness, as well as processes of a more cognitive kind such as differences in parent-child discourse concerning feelings and children's verbal ability or IQ, have all been suggested as key. We examined several of these possible antecedents in a study of 2- to 3-year-olds and found that separate, unique contributions to the variance in the outcome measures were made by several different features of the children's family experiences

(Dunn, Brown, Slomkowski, Tesla, & Youngblade, 1991). The frequency of mother-child conversations about feelings, for instance, was related to differences in children's understanding of emotions, and this contribution to the variance was separate from the contribution of differences in mother-child involvement.

In summary, the argument made here is that we need to broaden the framework within which we think about and measure children's relationships with their parents; we also must differentiate between different aspects of what is an extraordinarily rich and complex relationship, even when children are only preschoolers. The question of how such different aspects are related to differences in children's outcome is wide open for empirical inquiry. As a working hypothesis, it seems likely that different features of parent-child relationships are related to different aspects of children's later outcome. Security of attachment may well be related to aspects of the security of children's later relationships and the confidence and trust they feel in their closest relationships, as Bowlby and Ainsworth proposed. Note, however, that whereas Bowlby and Ainsworth argued for links between attachment quality and indindviduals' ability to form later intimate relationships, they did not propose that all aspects of later personality development or adjustment would be linked to differences in early attachment relationships (Ainsworth & Bowlby, 1991). Note also that the examples cited here have all concerned children of 18 months or older, whereas Bowlby and Ainsworth were chiefly concerned with even younger children. We need to account for such age differences: The developmental issues may well be important. For instance, the different dimensions of the relationship could be correlated when the babies are 1 year old but differentiated later.

A range of hypotheses could be made and tested. These include, for example, the idea that differences in parent-child discourse about feelings and the social world are related to the subtlety of children's social competence in later peer relationships, that the experience of shared humor is related to a later propensity to enjoy wit and lightheartedness in relationships, and that evaluative discourse in the relationship is related to later feelings of self-worth. Finally, to make progress in clarifying how early parent-child relationships affect later developments, we need to pit competing hypotheses against one another: we must include a study of alternative (and possibly complementary) approaches to the attachment approach, which is currently almost the only framework for understanding the developmental significance of parent-child relationships.

Developmental Change and Individual Differences in Parent-Child Relationships

Paradoxically, a second issue that remains relatively unexplored within an attachment framework concerns the significance of developmental changes in children for their relationships with their parents. Children change dramatically in their ability to understand the emotions and intentions of others, relationships between others, and the sanctions and social rules of their world, and in their communicative powers during the early years of childhood. Surely, these developments mean that their relationships will also change in significant ways. The chief focus of the attachment approach is on characteristics of the relationships that are believed to be largely "set" during the first 18 months or so of a child's life. Developmental changes in the expression of attachment are acknowledged and included in the assessments of the attachment relationships of 2- to 4-year-old children, but the underlying continuity of individual differences in the attachment status of children from late infancy is a key concept. Continuity is even sought between generations, and this clearly presents some major conceptual problems. Adult love relationships and parents' attachment to their children clearly differ in crucial respects from toddlers' dependencies on their parents. As attachment researchers themselves have noted, little attention has been paid to possible developmental changes in individual differences in quality of attachment (Crittenden, 1990), with the exception of the striking evidence that life events that affect the family can alter children's attachment status (Vaughn, Egeland, Sroufe, & Waters, 1979; see also the review in Lamb, Thompson, Gardner, & Charnov, 1985).

In contrast, a focus on other dimensions allows us to explore the question of how developmental changes in these early years affect the pattern of individual differences in parent-child relationships. The following important points emerge. (Note that we are again forced to discuss chiefly mothers rather than parents; studies of fathers are few and far between.)

1. Mothers respond differently to developmental changes in children's abilities and characteristics.

Two examples from recent longitudinal studies illustrate this point. First, in the Colorado Adoption Project we were able to compare the interaction between mothers and their successive children when each child was 12, 24, and 36 months old (Dunn & Plomin, 1986; Dunn, Plomin, & Daniels, 1986; Dunn, Plomin, & Nettles, 1985). We found that the mothers were quite consistent in how they behaved—in terms of affectionate, playful, and responsive behavior—to each of their two children at the same age, although little stability was seen in differences in the mothers' behavior to each individual child as he or she grew. In other words, a mother who was particularly responsive and affectionate to her 12-month-old was not, relative to the other mothers, particularly affectionate to that same child a year later; but she was relatively affectionate to her second child when that child reached 12 months. The children's particular stage of development had a surprisingly large effect on individual differences in mothers' behavior, at least in the circumstances in which we studied them. To put it crudely, some mothers seemed to be particularly "turned on" by their children as 1-year-olds and less affectionate, relative to other mothers, when they became argumentative 2- or 3-year-olds, while other mothers delighted especially in their children as they became talkative and engaging 2-year-olds. Thus, a new pattern of individual differences in mothers' affectionate responsive behavior became apparent as the children grew up. These results imply that key contributions to the changes in the pattern of individual differences in parent-child relationships were the differences in mothers' interest and responsiveness to the new developments in their children.

The same general point was made in a study in England that used quite a different methodology: long, naturalistic observations of mother-child pairs who were studied from the babies' birth until their first year at school (Bernal-Dunn & Richards, 1979). During the first year, clear and stable differences were found in mothers' responsiveness to their babies' crying and vocalizing; during the children's second year, however, as they began to talk, new patterns of differences in mothers' responsiveness became apparent. And it was these individual differences in mother-child interaction during the second year rather than in the first that predicted the children's later success on verbal and cognitive assessments.

2. The relative contribution of individual differences in children to the parent-child relationship changes with development.

As children grow up, their contribution to the balance of initiating and maintaining communication with their mothers changes, as Clarke-Stewart and Hevey showed in their study of children who were followed from 18 to 30 months of age (Clarke-Stewart & Hevey, 1981). Their growing ability to argue and to justify their actions verbally during their third year changes the patterns of control and conflict with their mothers in the family (Munn, 1989). Thus, the significance of individual differences in children's contributions to the dyadic relationship increases as they enter the third and fourth year. Again, this opens the possibility of considerable change in the individual differences in power relations and conflict management between parents and children. The Pennsylvania study showed that children become increasingly able to reason, justify, and excuse their own actions, as well as to understand the goals, feelings, and intentions of those with whom they are in conflict. Do these increases in social understanding lead to more harmony in parent-child relationships? Only in a few cases. Generally, the children we studied used these new skills to achieve their own ends, not to resolve conflict smoothly (Tesla & Dunn, 1992).

3. New dimensions of relationships emerge as children grow up.

One of the most striking developmental changes of the transition from infancy to early childhood is the growth of children's sense of self and their awareness of how others view them. The development of this self-consciousness allows new possibilities; for example, the parent-child relationship can be a resource for fostering a sense of self-competence and self-worth—or its opposite. With the development of children's capabilities for intimacy and self-disclosure and their understanding of the power of evaluative talk, new dimensions of individual differences in the parent-child relationship emerge.

4. The effect of the outside world on family relationships changes.

Any serious consideration of relationships must appreciate the links between those relationships and the social world. From birth, children are cultural creatures, and their relationships with their parents are influenced by the wider world beyond the family. It is not just parents whose behavior and perceptions reflect their cultural world: By 2 and 3 years of age, children's understanding of the social rules beyond the family colors their close relationships—and those rules differ in different cultures (Dunn & Brown, 1991). Furthermore, the links between social support and institutions beyond the family and the quality of family relationships change as children grow up; this implies that new patterns of individual differences in parent-child relationships may well emerge as children develop. The new influence of the peer group, of daycare or school experiences, and the growth of children's consciousness of the norms and expectations of the broader cultural world are likely to have different effects on individual children and parents. Consider, for example, the effects on some school-aged boys of peer-group pressure to be "macho." Here is how one mother in the Cambridge Sibling Study viewed the influence of the boys her son befriended at school:

> Since he's been at this school, with this group of boys—they're all trying to be so macho, you know—he's been different with me, and with her [his younger sister]. More sarcastic, superior, so into boy things—and trying to be "tough." He wants to be like them.

As a second example, consider young children from minority groups who start preschool or kindergarten in a cultural world dominated by the majority culture, whose values and expectations may differ notably from those of the minority families. The impact of a growing awareness of minority status and of the different expectations and beliefs of a majority culture may be very great for some children, and the effects of their experiences at school may well be carried home. Again, a new source of individual differences in parent-child relationships opens up.

The Strange Situation and Relationships

Several other conceptual issues raised by studies of attachment behavior deserve brief mention. One concerns an ambiguity in what exactly we can infer from the differences in children's behavior when they undergo the sequence of separations and reunions with their parents in a laboratory version of the Strange Situation. Do differences in attachment behavior as assessed in the Strange Situation reflect differences in the relationship between child and caregiver or differences in the children themselves? The Strange Situation was designed to capture relationship differences, yet attachment researchers have not always been precise about what is being measured. Often infants are the ones assigned to the categorization of secure (B babies), insecure-avoidant (A babies), or insecure-resistant (C babies) (e.g., Ainsworth, Blehar, Waters, & Wall, 1978; Sroufe & Waters, 1977).

But we should not assume that a child's behavior in the Strange Situation reflects either some dimension of insecurity that is a child characteristic or a permanent quality of the child-parent relationship. Evidence on the stability of attachment status shows that while Strange Situation behavior can be stable over time, when family circumstances change, so too does behavior in the Strange Situation (Vaughn et al., 1979). These findings have three important implications (Lamb et al., 1985). First, Strange Situation behavior tells us about the current status of the parent-child attachment security, not necessarily about earlier or later aspects of the relationship. Second, attachment security is not stable but is changeable. Third, predictions from Strange Situation behavior to later functioning will depend on continuity in family functioning; thus, in cases of such prediction we may well be tapping not so much a continuity in attachment security but continuity in other aspects of children's family relationships and social experiences.

A second set of problems in interpreting Strange Situation behavior is raised by the evidence that children from cultures other than the United States behave rather differently from American toddlers in the Strange Situation. For Japanese babies who have had very little experience in being separated from their mothers, the separations are extremely stressful—much more so than for most American babies. By contrast, the separations appear to be less stressful for German and Swedish babies than for American babies. Some researchers have argued that these differences suggest that factors other than maternal sensitivity have a strong effect on Strange Situation behavior, that prior experiences of separation profoundly affect the meaning of the Strange Situation for babies, and thus the "meaning" of their response to their mothers' disappearances and reappearances may also be very different for babies from these different cultures (Lamb et al., 1985). A note of caution here: The most recent evidence suggests that, at least in industrialized countries, within-country variance may be more than between-country variance (Van Ijzendoorn & Kroonenberg, 1988).

Research on daycare experiences and children's reaction to the Strange Situation has similar implications, namely, that children's experience of being separated from their mothers will have important effects on the meaning of the Strange Situation for young children (Clarke-Stewart, 1989). If children who are used to daily separations from their mothers when they are taken to daycare appear less emotionally upset by the Strange Situation, we cannot conclude that, in general, the security of their relationship with their parents is at risk.

A third issue in interpreting the Strange Situation concerns the categorization of the relationship into a simple three-way or four-way classification. Is this the most sensitive way to understand individual differences, even if we assume that it is appropriate to think of a single dimension of security in relationships? Notably, the categorization of Strange Situation behavior is often divided more than the simple A, B, and C of Ainsworth's original work; now the B category is further subdivided into four different subcategories, and category D includes a heterogeneous variety of "unclassifiable" responses from children, many of whom are considered to be disturbed on other criteria (e.g., Crittenden, 1988). The original notion of dividing children into those whose relationships were insecure or secure reflected a clinical concern, a need to identify those who were doing well with those who were not. It is almost a disease model. However, it is a dangerous assumption that insecure behavior in the Strange Situation reflects pathology. As Rutter (1991, p. 360) notes, "[I]t seems doubtful whether the Strange Situation procedure is sufficient on its own as a diagnostic tool; moreover, its validity is uncertain when used with infants with gross psychopathology, or with older children." For instance, one study of autistic children, who suffer from an extreme problem in their relationships, found that they did not differ from normal children in their Strange Situation behavior (Sigman & Ungerer, 1984).

The value of a dimensional rather than a categorical approach to describing individual differences in the security aspects of relationships recurs when we examine children's relationships with siblings and with peers—which also can include the provision of security in times of distress. Studying those relationships highlights how useful it is to view relationships in terms of the extent to which they provide security in stressful circumstances rather than in terms of a system in which some relationships are seen as "attachment relationships" and others are not.

A fourth problem in the interpretation of Strange Situation behavior becomes evident when we examine results of research on fathers. Consider the following three points:

1. Father-child attachment classification from the Strange Situation is reported to have no predictive power in relation to children's subsequent behavior in the preschool (Main, Kaplan, & Cassidy, 1985).

2. A valuable longitudinal study of mother-child and father-child attachment relationships reports no relation between father-child Strange Situation classification and Q-set assessments of their attachment (Youngblade, Park, & Belsky, submitted; see also Stevenson-Hinde & Shouldice, 1990, for parallel findings on mother-child relationships).

3. Currently, little published validity data is available on the relation of father-child Strange Situation classification to the children's and fathers' behavior at home (see, however, Cox, Owen, Henderson, & Margand, 1992, for evidence that fathers' parenting behavior at 3 months is associated with children's Strange Situation behavior toward fathers; fathers' sensitivity, animation in play, positive affect, and vocalization frequency were all related to secure attachment at 12 months).

One interpretation of these points that has been offered is that the Strange Situation may be a less adequate measure of infant-father than infant-mother relationships. Youngblade and her colleagues have suggested that if the role of the father is to provide the child with an entrée into the social world (e.g., Parsons & Bales, 1956), then "secure" behavior in the Strange Situation directed to the father can be considered enmeshed or dependent behavior, later covarying with less optimal behavior with peers.

In summary, these findings on crossnational daycare-homecare differences and father-child relationships and the concerns over how to interpret Strange Situation behavior bring home one general point. If we seriously wish to study either the security aspects of children's relationships with their parents or the other dimensions of these relationships, then we should develop a variety of alternatives to the Strange Situation as assessments. Undoubtedly, in other scientific domains researchers would not be content with a single measure—essentially, a dichotomy—in their attempts to capture something as complex as the relationship between child and parent.

Individual Differences in Children

We began in Chapter 1 with an emphasis on the links between the individual characteristics of both child and parent and the quality of their relationship, links that are key to a full description of the relationship. And implicit in each point concerning developmental change outlined above, as well as in the findings on crossnational and daycare differences in experience, is that we must pay serious attention to individual differences in children and their contribution to differences in their relationships with their parents. However, in both parenting literature and attachment research, the focus has been chiefly on the influence of differences in parental rather than child behavior, personality, or beliefs. In both literatures, differences in maternal personality and mother-child interaction in the early years are indeed frequently correlated with child outcome measures such as children's interactive behavior with peers. (The matter of what causal mechanisms we can infer from these correlations is discussed in Chapter 6.) To what extent do differences between children also contribute to the various dimensions of the relationship between child and parent that we have discussed?

Individual Differences in Attachment

Within the great bulk of attachment research, individual differences in the quality of the relationship are attributed to differences in maternal sensitivity and responsiveness over the previous months. A repeated finding in longitudinal studies of attachment is that children whose mothers scored high on measures of positive responsiveness and sensitivity were more likely to behave as if their relationship was secure in the Strange Situation. Parallel findings for fathers were reported by Cox and her colleagues; no assessment of how children's behavior or temperament were related to the fathers' behavior was included (Cox et al., 1992). This emphasis on the mother as the source of differences in children's security fits, of course, with the psychoanalytic foundations of attachment theory. But the evidence for links between differences in mothers' behavior and subsequent mother-child relationship differences does not mean that differences between children do not also contribute to the quality of the relationship. Indeed, we should remember that the very differences between mothers that are emphasized in attachment research may in part be a response to differences between children: Recall that principle underlined by Hinde. To any parent with more than one child, the idea that differences in their relationships with their various children are attributable solely to parent differences is hard to reconcile with their own experience of the impact of their children's individual differences on other family members.

The last decade has seen controversy about the extent to which young children's behavior in the Strange Situation is influenced by characteristics of their personality or temperament. Some researchers have argued, for instance, that differences in Strange Situation behavior reflect temperamental differences in response to stress rather than attachment security (Kagan, 1982), and that differences in temperament in interaction with differences in parent-child relationships or previous experiences can contribute to attachment quality (Goldsmith, Bradshaw, & Rieser-Danner, 1986; Thompson, Connell, & Bridges, 1988). However, others cite the evidence for lack of concordance between how a child behaves in the Strange Situation with respect to father and mother as evidence against the view that the Strange Situation indeed taps personality differences; to them, it supports the view that what is measured is a relationship quality.

Two separate points are at issue here. One is the matter of how far differences in children's behavior in the Strange Situation are attributable to temperamental differences in the children rather than relationship differences. The second is the matter of how we interpret differences between children's behavior with their fathers and with their mothers.

The temperament issue is not yet resolved. A helpful rapprochement between the two positions is laid out by Belsky and Rovine (1988), who provide evidence that temperamental differences do contribute to the different ways in which children behave under the stress of the Strange Situation—*and* that broad differences in the security dimension are also evident. A recent examination of six separate studies conducted in the United States, Canada, and England, which used the Attachment Q Sort and temperament data, reports the existence of "consistent, and developmentally increasing, associations between attachment security and a temperament dimension reflecting negative emotionality and/or affect activation" (Vaughn, Stevenson-Hinde, Waters, Kotsaftis, Lefever, Shouldice, Trudel, & Belsky, 1992). The authors suggest that when attachment is assessed from a Q Sort and reflects day-to-day functioning rather than children's responses to the stressful Strange Situation, then the overlap with temperamental differences is greater than in the latter situation. (This greater agreement could well be expected because they are both based on maternal perceptions; see, for example, Hinde & Tobin, 1986; Stevenson-Hinde & Shouldice, 1990.)

On the issue of children's behavior with their fathers and mothers in the Strange Situation, note that even if clear differences are seen in children's relationships with their two parents, this does not mean that temperamental characteristics are unimportant in contributing to those different relationships. Clearly, different temperamental dimensions can be important in different relationships, and little overlap may be seen in the dimensions that are significant for a child's various relationships (see, for example, Hinde, Tamplin, & Barrett, in press a, b).

In any case, the basic point that children behave significantly differently with their mothers and fathers in the Strange Situation is still open to question. A recent meta-analysis of 11 studies that included children with both parents reports some similarity in Strange Situation behavior with the two parents—even within the subgroup classification of the secure category (Fox, Kimmerly, & Schafer, 1991). Several different interpretations of this similarity are possible. We could conclude that babies behave in a similar way to their mothers and their fathers because, as some attachment theorists would predict, the situation actually measures the child's "internal working model" of relationships that he or she has formed with the principal attachment figure, which leads the child to behave as if secure in relationships with others.

A second interpretation also suggested by Fox and his colleagues is that the Strange Situation "assesses the history of interaction, the family situation, and environment. Parents may be similar in their caregiving behavior and value systems, regarding issues important to secure attachment such as responsivity and sensitivity to infant cues" (Fox et al., 1991, p. 222). In fact, the whole issue of how far mothers and fathers differ in their responsiveness to their babies remains unsettled. Although one study reports similarities of mother and father responsiveness in the first year (Belsky & Volling, 1987), many others of father-child and mother-child interaction in the first year report differences in interaction (Belsky, Gilstrap, & Rovine, 1984; Parke, 1978; Parke & Sawin, 1980), while others report differences in the values and caregiving expectations of mothers and fathers and differences between parents in their description of their children's temperament (Frodi, Lamb, Frodi, Hwang, Forrstrom, & Corry, 1982).

A third interpretation, which is not incompatible with the other possibilities, is that children's temperament does contribute to the Strange Situation behavior (and thus to the similarity in behavior to mother and father). Fox and his colleagues cite evidence for stability over the first year in babies' reactions to frustrating circumstances (Fox, 1989; Stifter & Fox, 1990) and in their propensity to play with toys and avoid people (Lewis & Feiring, 1989). A cautious conclusion would be that temperamental differences between children contribute in a modest way to behavior in the Strange Situation (Goldsmith & Alansky, 1987; Thompson, Connell, & Bridges, 1988; Vaughn, Lefever, Seifer, & Barglow, 1989), although, of course, they are not the only influence. The development of insecure relationships as reflected in Strange Situation behavior is likely to be influenced by a range of circumstances: when parents are under stress, suffering from personality problems, or are without social support, or when children's personality characteristics themselves contribute to the difficulties parents have. These various factors may indeed interact: One study reports, for instance, that insecure attachments were more likely to develop in mother-child pairs in which the baby was particularly irritable and the mother had very little close support from her spouse or others (Crockenberg, 1981).

Differences in Other Dimensions
of Parent-Child Relationships

Within the other dimensions of parent-child relationships that we have discussed, individual differences in children clearly contribute to the quality of the relationship. A comparison of the parent-child relationships of different children within the same family makes this point clear. Our studies in England and in the United States show that both mother-child and father-child relationships can differ markedly for different children within the same family in warmth and in patterns of conflict and discipline. Figure 2.1 illustrates some of these differences for the mother-child pairs in the Colorado Sibling Study: The data from both observations and interviews with the mothers themselves showed, for the majority of mothers, differences in the affection they felt and in the control they engaged in with their two children.

Differences in children's temperament contribute to such differences (Dunn & Plomin, 1990). And the same mother can have a relationship with one child in which humor is a key theme but a relationship with another that is much less lighthearted, according to both the evidence of direct observations of the families and the mothers' own reports. Here is a quotation from a mother talking about her relationship with her secondborn child, Martin, aged 36 months, and his 5-year-old sister, Caroline:

> I just don't have the same jokey time with Caroline as I do with him. She takes everything more seriously, and we can't seem to laugh off our disagreements the way Martin and I do. With him, everything is a riot—even when I'm trying to get him dressed. He's always been a joker. With her, I have to tread so carefully.

We analyzed the jokes between the family members in this Cambridge study when the children were 36 months old, and the results showed that the majority of the humorous exchanges were initiated by or focused on these 3-year-old children themselves, who turned out to be central figures in the family jokes. The

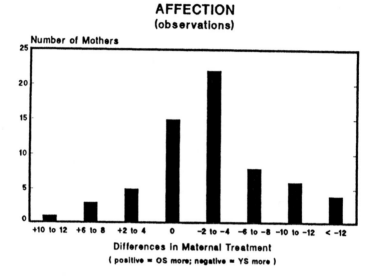

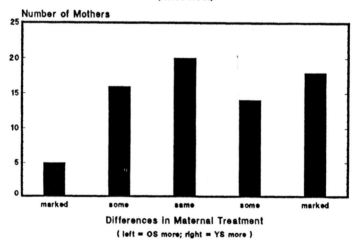

Figure 2.1. Relative Differences in Maternal Behavior Toward Siblings in the Colorado Sibling Study (from "Nonshared experiences within the family: Correlates of behavior problems in the middle childhood" by J. Dunn, C. Stocker, & R. Plomin, *Development and Psychopathology, 2,* pp. 113-126. Copyright 1990 by Cambridge University Press).

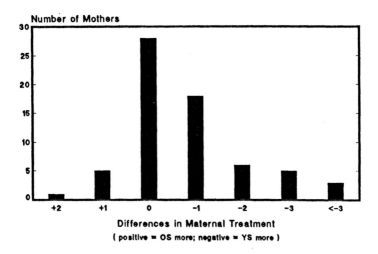

CONTROL
(observations)

Differences in Maternal Treatment
(positive = OS more; negative = YS more)

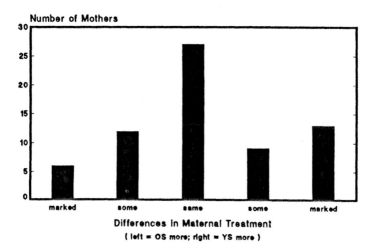

CONTROL/DISCIPLINE
(interview)

Differences in Maternal Treatment
(left = OS more; right = YS more)

Figure 2.1. Continued

differences between the children in their propensity to make jokes were linked to temperament differences, as other studies of older children have also reported (McGhee, 1989).

Differences between mother-child pairs in the frequency and nature of their communication about feelings and their discourse about self and others are also clearly related to individual differences between children—for example, differences in cognitive sophistication and verbal ability (Dunn et al., 1991). These associations between parent-child relationship differences and differences between children in cognitive ability or temperament raise another major issue about the origins of differences in relationships: the role of genetics. We must recognize that many of the aspects of parental behavior that we have discussed—for instance, parental warmth, involvement, and responsiveness—as well as the characteristics of the children that are associated with differences in relationship quality, appear to be related to genetic factors. For example, several studies have found that genetics contribute to parental warmth and supportiveness (Plomin & Bergeman, 1991). Children's temperament and IQ are also linked to heredity. It appears likely that the dimensions of shared feelings and self-disclosure, connectedness, and shared humor also will be influenced genetically. This point—that the quality of both parents' and children's behavior toward one another might involve genetic differences among parents and children—may at first seem surprising. However, it has far-reaching implications for thinking about the connections between relationships, and we will return to it in Chapter 5. We turn now to children and their siblings and to the complex relationships that they develop with one another.

Sibling Relationships

The striking differences between sibling pairs in their relationships are clear even to the most casual observer. Some brothers and sisters appear affectionate and concerned, real friends to one another. Others are constantly in conflict, even coming to blows. Yet others appear uninterested, uninvolved with each other, and they very much go their separate ways. Tina and her sister, mentioned in the first chapter, were extremely close and affectionate, while Nat and his brother quarreled relentlessly.

The results of systematic research confirm this picture of great variation in the different dimensions of siblings' relationships. On every aspect of sibling interaction or sibling relationships that has been assessed, studies report a wide range of individual differences (Boer & Dunn, 1992). These dramatic differences raise a host of questions for parents who worry about whether it is their fault if their children do not get along well and what this portends for their future. Sibling conflict tops the list of family problems that parents bring to professionals (Baskett & Johnson, 1982; Clifford, 1959; Newson & Newson, 1970), and the differences in how siblings get along raise questions both for clinicians, faced with the shaping role of aggressive children on their siblings (Patterson, 1984, 1986), and for psychologists or family systems theorists who are concerned with understanding the patterns of relationships within the family (Minuchin, 1985). The focus of much of this attention is on the negative, hostile aspects of the relationship, but this concentration on rivalry and conflict does not adequately reflect the nature of individual differences between siblings. How can the qualities of siblings' relationships be described more fully?

Dimensions of Difference

With the exception of a classic series of studies by Helen Koch (1960), the relationship between siblings was ignored by scientists for a surprisingly long time, given the developmental significance accorded to child-child interaction by major theorists (e.g., Piaget, 1965; Sullivan, 1953) and to sibling rivalry by clinicians and personality theorists (e.g., Adler, 1959; Freud, 1949). Approximately 10 years ago, systematic studies of siblings began to appear in the literature, although much of this research focused on infancy and early childhood and on observations of the interaction between siblings rather than on broad relationship dimensions (Dunn, 1983). Recent studies have shown an increased interest in describing relationships, including a focus on the perceptions of siblings and their parents concerning the relationship, and a welcome increase also has been seen in studies of siblings in both middle childhood and adolescence (Buhrmester, 1992; Furman & Buhrmester, 1985; Raffaelli, 1991). The particular dimensions that researchers choose to describe the relationship vary with their theoretical perspective, although many similarities are seen across studies in the general patterns they describe. Among the dimensions of relationships described for siblings are both interesting similarities with those described for the relationship between parent and child and intriguing differences.

RIVALRY

Rivalry between siblings is probably the dimension of sibling relationships that has received most attention historically, because of the supposition that this is one key to later personality differences (Freud, 1949). Clearly, rivalry is a relevant and important dimension in many sibling relationships. Most parents discern some element of rivalry in their children's relationships, and observations of young siblings confirm how promptly they react to any attention that a sibling gets from shared parents (Kendrick & Dunn, 1982). However, recent research indicates that rivalry should not be thought of simply as one pole of a unitary dimension, with friendly cooperation at one end and rivalry at the other. Rather, many studies report two relatively independent positive and negative dimensions, whether the source of the information is maternal interview, interviews with the siblings themselves, or direct observation. The independence of these dimensions is evident in the different combinations of hostility and friendliness to be found in different sibling pairs. Some siblings are both quarrelsome and frequent playmates, others are low on both negative and friendly dimensions, while other pairs are high on one or the other dimension.

Studies of school-aged children further suggest that we can distinguish separate dimensions of *rivalry, conflict, control,* and *friendliness* (Furman & Buhrmester, 1985). Some uncertainty, however, remains about whether separate dimensions of rivalry and conflict can be reliably distinguished in younger children, although the extent of conflict between two siblings is not closely related to their affection, cooperation, and support of each other. Indeed, among preschool-aged siblings the children who frequently enter into conflict with their siblings have been found to be particularly likely to attempt to share, help, and cooperate (Dunn & Munn, 1986). This pattern parallels findings on young children playing with their peers at preschool or daycare: Conflicts between friends are just as frequent as those between children who are nonfriends (Hartup, 1989; Radke-Yarrow, Zahn-Waxler, & Chapman, 1983). The range of differences between sibling pairs in conflict is very striking: In our current study of 50 Pennsylvania families, the frequency of conflict incidents between the siblings ranged from 0 to 56 conflict episodes per hour when children were 33 months old. However, for most brothers and sisters, the relationship clearly is far more complex and more rewarding for both children than a focus solely on the negative aspects would suggest.

ATTACHMENT SECURITY

That some children are attached to one another is evident very early in the sibling relationship; they are reported by their mothers to miss their sibling in his or her absence, to be transformed with happiness and delight when the sibling reappears, and to use the sibling as a base from which they happily explore novel places (Dunn & Kendrick, 1982). Siblings have also been studied in the Strange Situation, and here, children of 4 years of age can act as sources of attachment security for an infant sibling (Stewart & Marvin, 1984; Teti & Ablard, 1989). For some, but not all, toddlers, the relationship with an older sibling apparently includes a dimension of attachment security. Incidentally, these results provide evidence that supports the shift in attachment theory from viewing attachment as a dimension of the caregiver-child relationship to seeing it as a quality that may be present in several different relationships—even that between a 1-year-old and a 4-year-old.

CONNECTEDNESS, SELF-DISCLOSURE, AND HUMOR

Just as these "verbal" dimensions turn out to be relevant, measurable, and revealing of differences between parent-child dyads, they also are appropriate for describing aspects of the relationships between siblings in childhood. Consider, for example, the dimension of connectedness or coherence of communication. In some sibling pairs, the cohesion of their communication is very marked. In others, the two children rarely converse and play in a connected way. In our current Pennsylvania study, for example, the differences between sibling pairs in the proportion of their conversation that was "connected" ranged from only 18% of their conversational turns to 100% (Slomkowski & Dunn, 1992). Much— but not all—of this connected conversation was friendly; the differences reflect differences in the extent to which siblings are "on the same wavelength."

In shared humor, we also find wide differences between siblings (McGhee, 1989). These are particularly vivid, because shared jokes between siblings tend to focus on rather different topics from those of parent and child. For some siblings, dirty jokes and amusement at violations of appropriate or polite behavior are a continuous source of shared pleasure. Often when the younger sibling is still a toddler or young preschooler, the older sibling takes a leading role in making these daring jokes, reducing the younger sibling to hysterical laughter. Ritual word play and verbal insults also form a continuing thread that runs through the conversation of some sibling pairs, and they are a form of joint humor that is missing from parent-child relationships but is common between peers (Garvey, 1977). In the following example, 2-year-old Laura and her older sister engage in ritual chanting—and then Laura delightedly introduces a variant of the repeated pattern:

Sib: Hello, Lollipop Laura!
Laura: Hello, Lollipop!
Sib: Hello, Lollipop Laura!
Laura: Hello, Lollipop!
Sib: Hello, Lollipop you!
Laura: Hello, Lollipop!
Sib: Hello, Lollipop Laura!
Laura: Hello, Lollipop BUM!

The range of differences between families in the frequency of shared humor and jokes between the siblings was marked. In the Pennsylvania study, for example, the frequency of jokes between siblings ranged from none to 7 an hour, and some of these sibling jokes could be quite extended.

The dimension of shared self-disclosure and discussion of feelings that formed a thread in many parent-child relationships is also found among some siblings—but is extremely rare in others. In one important respect, these conversations about feelings between siblings differ from those between parents and children: Children discuss the sibling's feelings much more than they do their parents' feelings: three times more frequently in our Pennsylvania families, in fact (Brown & Dunn, 1992). So, for those sibling pairs who have such discussions frequently, they form an important forum for learning about the feelings of another. In this context, note that a recent study reports children with siblings performing with much greater success on tests of understanding "other minds" than do singletons (Perner, Ruffman, & Leekham, submitted), a provocative finding that deserves attention if replicated. The range of individual differences between sibling pairs in such discussions about feelings is as marked as the differences between mother-child pairs: The range of discussions about feelings between siblings in families in our Pennsylvania sample is from none to as many as 32 conversational turns per hour.

SHARED FANTASY

Other features of the relationship between siblings are found less frequently in parent-child relationships. A particularly striking feature of some siblings' relationships is shared fantasy. In two separate studies of preschool-aged siblings, one in the United States and one in England, we have found that between one quarter and one third of the studied sibling pairs engaged in frequent and sustained joint fantasy play (Dunn & Dale, 1984; Youngblade & Dunn, submitted). Unlike the joint pretend games in which mothers and children joined together (and mothers typically acted as didactic spectators, instructing their children on how it is in the real world), in fantasy play both siblings frequently acted as full partners in the shared pretend world. With little instruction or "framing" of the game needed, both children usually slipped into the shared fantasy world and negotiated the course of play. To manage such a transition into a joint fantasy with another person reflects a relatively sophisticated understanding of a shared, make-believe world—impressive intellectual sharing for children of 2 and 3 years of age.

Three general points stand out from the studies of shared pretend play between young siblings. First, children can engage in such play extremely early, when it is set up by a friendly and supportive sibling. Thus, we found that even 18-month-olds, in the context of a warm relationship with a sibling, participated in role games (Dunn & Dale, 1984). In one of our Cambridge studies, six of forty 18-month-olds took part in such games, with their older sibling setting up the play.

Second, marked developmental changes in siblings' participation in this shared fantasy are evident in the early years; between 24 and 30 months, for example, we find striking increases in the innovative contributions and the negotiations made by the younger sibling to the joint make-believe. As illustration, consider a sequence of mother-baby play in one of our Cambridge studies between 30-month-old Annie and her older sister, Carol. This was not an unusually long or complex sequence for this pair of sisters, and yet it lasted 140 conversational turns. Annie, in her role as Baby, made the following contributions to the narrative of the play:

Makes babbling noises.
Crawls.
Says she cannot put slippers on: "I'm baby."
Designates a "baby bed."
Asks for porridge.
Plays guitar in a way she designates as "a baby way. . . . Me babby."
Addresses sibling as "Mummy."
Acts "naughty" with guitar.
Pretends to get lost.
Snores.
"Cries," and in answer to sibling asking why she is crying ("What's wrong, Babbu?"), replies "Me can't get to sleep."
Instructs sibling on what she should say in her role as Mummy.

These innovative actions were all accepted by Carol, who was "Mummy" in the game. Between 18 and 30 months, Annie had also become less compliant about her older sister's directions in the shared pretend, so in this one sequence of make-believe she was noncompliant and critical in the following ways:

When told to babble like a baby and not to cry, she cried.
She criticized her sibling's action in terms of role: "No, you not a baby."
She denied that what she was pretending to drink was a milk shake.

She denied that they were both tired in the game.
She refused to go on "Mummy's" knee.

The third general point is that for those sibling pairs who joined in cooperating in make-believe, this play was a riveting, absorbing activity for both children. Both children picked up on the play mood of the other with great sensitivity, coordinated their actions, and shared the collective symbolism of their pretend world. We might think this an aspect of relationships that just characterizes siblings in the early years of childhood. Not so: Our follow-up of the Cambridge families into middle childhood and early adolescence showed that even as 10- to 13-year-olds some of these siblings still enjoyed a shared fantasy world. The form was a little different: Several pairs had secret dens and gangs, and some wrote stories together about their fantasy lives (shades of the Brontes!); however, the siblings were adamant that this shared fantasy was a key part of their relationship.

What are the links between the different aspects of friendly positive behavior between siblings? Siblings who engage in frequent joint fantasy are likely to show interest and friendliness toward one another in other ways (Dunn & Dale, 1984; Youngblade & Dunn, submitted). Joint pretend depends on a close matching of interests and an attunement to the other that is rarely achieved unless siblings are affectionate, it seems. But when we look closely at other different kinds of positive behavior—helpfulness, sharing, concern about distress—it appears that for young siblings there are few links between individual differences in these various qualities and the dimension of shared fantasy. Those siblings who share and help each other or who are concerned at each other's distress are not necessarily those who join in cooperative play together (Dunn & Munn, 1986). No single dimension of prosocial behavior in the relationships of young siblings seems to exist; different motivations may underlie caring for a distressed sibling and joining in a shared fantasy (see Eisenberg & Hand, 1979, for similar findings for peers). Given the ambivalence that frequently characterizes the relationship, we should not be surprised that some sibling pairs cooperate frequently and yet are not concerned by each other's distress.

Interestingly, we also found in the Pennsylvania study that "connectedness" of communication, negative affect, and lack of involvement were all dimensions that were independent from the dimension of cooperation and shared fantasy, and from each other. These dimensions were not only uncorrelated, but also showed different patterns of association with the various measures of child outcome that we examined. For instance, success on the assessments of understanding emotions and "other minds" was associated with the experience of frequent cooperative play with the older sibling, not with the expression of frequent positive or negative affect or with a high degree of involvement (Dunn, Brown, Slomkowski, Tesla, & Youngblade, 1991; Youngblade & Dunn, submitted).

RECIPROCITY, COMPLEMENTARITY, AND THE BALANCE OF SIBLING RELATIONSHIPS

The parent-child relationship is often described as a complementary one in which parent and child take different but dependent roles (Hinde, 1979) rather than as a relationship in which both partners take reciprocal, matching roles as, for instance, in those between close friends who enjoy balanced, equitable relations. One of the distinctive general features of sibling relationships is that they can include both complementary and reciprocal features (Dunn, 1983). Because one child is older, more developmentally advanced, and may be assigned caregiving tasks and be expected to take responsibility for the younger, the relationship can at times resemble a parent-child relationship in the balance of power and nurturance between the two children. But they can also interact as more equal partners, as when they joke together and negotiate with equity the course of shared pretend.

Sibling pairs can differ, then, in the degree to which their relationship has complementary and reciprocal features, and the overall quality of their relationship may be affected by the balance of these two sets of features. And this raises the issue of the extent to which two siblings have similar or different experiences within the relationship. No one doubts that the relationship between a parent and child is experienced differently by each participant; in any "complementary" relationship, the two partners will inevitably have rather different experiences. Even within a marriage, the relationship can be experienced quite differently by the two partners: "His" and "her" marriages are common (Bernard, 1982). Yet most attempts to study sibling relationships have focused on the dimensions of conflict, rivalry, companionship, and affection as if they were experienced similarly by both children in the relationship. But does this reflect the real state of affairs?

Recent years have seen a new surge of interest in whether and how markedly siblings have different perceptions of their own relationship and different experiences within that relationship. As we noted in Chapter 1, behavioral geneticists have shown that the significant sources of environmental influence on individual differences in many aspects of personality and adjustment work *within* rather than *between* families (Plomin & Daniels, 1987; Scarr & Grajek, 1982). Family influence works to make siblings different, not similar, and the salient sources of influence that affect development are specific to each child in a family rather than shared. This evidence implies that if we are to explain the development of individual differences in general, we must explain why children growing up within the same family are notably different from one another. As part of the search to identify these salient sources of different environmental experience, researchers have shown increasing interest in the different experiences that siblings have within a family. Two possible sources of such different experiences, for example, have been systematically explored: differences in parent-child relationships and different experiences within the sibling relationship itself. How differently do young siblings view their experience within the relationship? And how differently are they seen to behave toward one another?

Evidence from interview, questionnaire, and observation studies shows that differences in siblings' experience of friendliness, hostility, and affection within the "same" relationship are marked (these studies are summarized in Dunn & Plomin, 1990). Particularly vivid are accounts by the children themselves. Compare the following sets of comments made by a pair of siblings in the Cambridge Sibling Study about their relationship.

Nancy (age 10) about her brother Carl: "Well, he's nice to me. And he sneaks into my bed at night time from Mummy. I think I'd be very lonely without Carl. I play with him a lot and he thinks up lots of ideas and it's very exciting. He comes and meets me at the gate after school and I think that's very friendly. . . . He's very kind. . . . Don't really know what I'd do without a brother."

Carl (age 6) talks about Nancy: "She's pretty disgusting and we don't talk to each other much. I don't really know much about her." [Interviewer: "What is it you particularly like about her?"] "Nothing. Sometimes when I do something wrong she tells me off quite cruelly."

When we examined a rating of affective closeness in relationships that was based on the children's descriptions of the relationship in an open-ended interview, the results showed that only 23% of children expressed similar degrees of closeness on the rating scale. A second study examined parents' views of the siblings' friendliness and hostility and found that parents rated 60% of the children as different from their siblings in the extent and expression of their positive feelings for their sibling. For conflict and hostility, there was more mutuality in the relationship; even so, 40% of the siblings were perceived by their mothers as differing in hostility. A dimension of mutuality could then also be used to describe differences between these siblings pairs in the extent to which they share common experiences in the relationship.

Developmental Changes

One basic set of questions looms large for parents: Do the individual differences in sibling relationships that are so marked in early years continue as the children grow up? Will they always fight this way? Will the affection and support that is so touching to see continue as they both become part of a larger world of school and friends?

Over the early years, when both children in a sibling pair are developing rapidly, interesting changes take place in the pattern of individual differences in sibling relationships. For example, as secondborn siblings grow from 18 to 36 months old, they take a much more active and initiatory role in the relationship, and thus the contribution of the younger sibling's individual characteristics comes to play a more substantial part in the relationship over this period (Dunn & Munn, 1989). Data from the Cambridge Sibling Study showed that when the younger sibling was 24 months old, the establishment of joint play was correlated only with the temperament of the older sibling; by the time the younger sibling was 36 months of age, this play also was correlated with differences in the temperament of the younger sibling.

A similar picture of the increasing contribution of secondborn siblings to the dyadic relationship as they grow up—and the increasing time that siblings spend in talking and playing as the second child grows from a 2-year-old to a 4-year-old—comes from our analyses of the Pennsylvania study (Brown & Dunn, 1991). For instance, consider the changing patterns of communication about feelings. By 4 years of age, the secondborn children had become more interesting companions for their older siblings, and indeed they spent more time talking and playing with their older siblings than with their parents. Again, the implication is that we may get a shift in the pattern of individual differences in dyadic relationship measures as the secondborn child becomes more influential in the relationship—or at least more assertive.

What about stability in the quality of the relationship over the longer term? The first two studies that have followed siblings from early through middle childhood (the Colorado Sibling Study and the Cambridge Sibling Study) tell quite similar stories. For both the positive and negative aspects of the relationship, individual differences show positive correlations, but these are not notably strong. For example, in the Cambridge Sibling Study, the correlations over the 4-year period between the younger siblings' third and seventh years ranged from $r(40) = .42$ to .60 for the positive aspects of the relationship and from $r(40) = .29$ to .43 for the negative aspects. Although we could emphasize the stability that these correlations represent, they are not very high, and clearly many sibling pairs show marked changes in their relationships as they progress from the preschool to middle childhood periods. For the Colorado siblings, the average correlations over a 4-year period were $r(77) = .46$ for the positive aspects of the relationship and $r(77) = .39$, both significant at $p < 05$.

Important general lessons can be drawn from these changes in individual differences over time. First, even if a sibling relationship is close, harmonious, and conflict-free in the early years, this does not ensure a continuing happy relationship in middle childhood and adolescence, as we might expect if we thought children formed an "internal working model" of their sibling relationship in early childhood that was developmentally significant.

Second, the changes in sibling relationships highlight the importance of the wider social context in which children are growing up, especially the impact of life events in influencing individual differences in sibling relationships. For example, research shows that following divorce, the presence of a stepfather is related to poor sibling relationships (Hetherington, 1988). And in our studies of siblings in both Cambridge and Colorado, we find that negative life events were related to the quality of the siblings' relationships. In the Cambridge families, for example, life events were associated with increased warmth between the siblings.

Third, normative life events, such as the transition to secondary school of one sibling or other school changes, may affect the relationship between the two. The longitudinal data in the Cambridge study show that the impact of school and peer experiences varies. In some cases, the children and their mothers reported that their new friendships, their academic successes, and their enjoyment of a wider social world caused trouble in their sibling relationships. Children were quite often jealous and resentful of their siblings' successes in the school world. Here are one mother's comments on the changes that accompanied her second child's successful adjustment to a new school:

> When Ruth was miserable at school and being bullied, Clare stood up for her very much. . . . Clare sorted out the situation in her own way! And they stuck together very closely at school. . . . They didn't get on so well when Ruth started going to the Junior School. Because

Ruth made friends, and got some really super reports and she got a lot more confident—and instead of doing exactly what Clare said, and being bossed around, she started asserting herself, and we had a few crisis points then! [Laughs]. . . . I think that Clare is looking at her less as "her little sister" now, and they've both got very separate friends who are totally different types of children.

And here is an older sister's view of her younger brother's success:

I'm getting on really well with him at the moment, but a year or so ago when we both went to the same school I wasn't, 'cos there was a bit of competition, 'cos in our mathwork he moved up ahead of me. . . . It was really nasty.

Her brother also attributed the change in their relationship to the changes in their schools. "We really hated each other for a bit. . . . I think it's changed a lot with the school move." In other cases, children who have difficulties at new schools bring their unhappiness home, and their sibling relationships become increasingly negative. A third pattern is that children who have made a successful change to a new school become more confident; according to their mothers, this change makes them easier for everyone in the family to get along with. Although the particular patterns vary, the general point of some importance is the issue highlighted by Hinde's model: Salient influences on sibling relationships may be felt from social contexts beyond the family.

Individual Differences

Beyond the influences on changes in relationships, what other factors contribute to differences in the relations between siblings? First, as with parent-child relationships, the temperament of both the individuals in the relationship is important. Conflict between siblings, for instance, has been repeatedly found to be related to the temperament of the siblings in a dyad. Children who are active, intense, or unadaptable in temperament have more conflicted relationships with their siblings (Boer, 1990; Brody & Stoneman, 1987; Brody, Stoneman, & Burke, 1987; Stocker, Dunn, & Plomin, 1989). And the match between siblings in temperament is also important, with more conflict in sibling pairs who are very different in temperament (Munn & Dunn, 1989). This is an important point that will recur in the book: The temperament of both siblings is important in their dyadic relationship, and the match (or mismatch) between their temperaments is key to how they get along. And again, it reminds us that genetic influence may play a part in sibling relationships, affecting the quality of their relationship.

Less clear is the influence of the gender and age gap between siblings. With young siblings, the research findings are inconsistent and show relatively few links between such variables and the hostility or friendliness of siblings (Dunn, 1988b; Stoneman, Brody, & McKinnon, 1984; Teti, Bond, & Gibbs, 1986; Teti, Gibbs, & Bond, 1989). In contrast, family constellation variables apparently can affect siblings' relationships in middle childhood in complex ways (Buhrmester, 1992; Buhrmester & Furman, 1990). Whether these differences in findings mean that gender, birth position, and age gap become more important as siblings grow up is not clear. What is unquestionable is that individual differences in sibling relationship dimensions are closely connected to differences in parent-child, parent-sibling, and marital relationships; the connections between these relationships are considered in Chapter 5. We turn next to the close relationships that children form with other children outside the family—their friends.

Young Children's Friendships

Children's relations with other children outside the family range from passing acquaintance-ship to intense friendships. They include intimate, affectionate, dyadic relationships; detached and not-so-detached daily classroom exchanges with peers; and problematic bully-victim relationships. They also include membership—which can be central or peripheral—in larger groups of peers. The idea that these early peer relationships are developmentally important has a key place in the writings of Piaget (1965) and other theorists (e.g., Sullivan, 1953), and the last decade has witnessed a huge increase in studies of children with their peers (for recent reviews, see Asher & Coie, 1989; Berndt & Ladd, 1989; Dunn & McGuire, 1992; Parker & Asher, 1987; see also Gottman & Parker, 1986). Some researchers have argued that peer relationships play a special role in several areas of development, including fundamental social skills such as conflict resolution and perspective-taking (e.g., Hartup, 1983), moral understanding (Damon, 1977), and sex roles (Fine, 1980). Some also have suggested that such relationships are of particular importance in the development of children's sense of self (Sullivan, 1953) and that troubled peer relationships are associated with both concurrent and later adjustment problems (e.g., Parker & Asher, 1987).

The great bulk of research on peers that examines these ideas has focused not on relationships, but on the extent to which children are liked or disliked by their peers—the sociometrics of the classroom—or on the social behavior of individuals. But recently, the importance of the distinction between friendships and the popular regard of groups of peers has gained attention, and the need to move toward a relationships perspective in studying peers has been increasingly urged (Berndt & Ladd, 1989; Hinde, 1990). What do we know of the friendships of very young children and of the nature and significance of individual differences in such friendships?

Researchers used to assume that children younger than 6 or 7 had very limited abilities to relate to other children in an intimate way (e.g., Sullivan, 1953) and that friendship in early childhood was inevitably fleeting and transitory (Selman, 1980). Both of these views have now been qualified in important respects. First, although major increases in the extent and depth of intimacy between friends as children grow through middle childhood and adolescence are clear (e.g., Berndt & Perry, 1986), the new perspective on children's social understanding has shown that they have, even during the toddler years, some understanding of and sensitivity to the feelings and intentions of others; furthermore, these powers of understanding other people grow rapidly during the early childhood years. As we will see, some young children bring considerable powers of understanding, sensitivity, and intimacy to their relationships with close friends in early childhood.

Second, the view that young children's friendships are very unstable is not supported by recent evidence from longitudinal studies. For instance, a landmark study of friendship in preschool children by Howes (1987) found that children tended to maintain their friendships over a 2-year period, and for some children friendships lasted considerably longer. In our own research in Pennsylvania, the average length of time that 4-year-old children had been close friends was 2 years (see also Park, Lay, & Ramsay, 1990, for evidence on stability of young children's friendships). Another study of preschool children reported that more than one half of preschool-aged children had reciprocated friendships, and more than two-thirds of these friendships were stable over a 6-month period (Gershman & Hayes, 1983). Of course, the length of these friendships may well be influenced by the propinquity of children who share the same neighborhood over time, although, as parents know, propinquity by no means guarantees friendship.

Observational research shows that children's interactions with their friends differ from those with children who are not their friends in several ways. For instance, they spend more time interacting with their friends (Hartup, 1989), and their behavior in conflict differs: They are more likely to attempt conciliation with friends, although they may actually quarrel more with them than with nonfriends (Hartup, Laursen, Stewart, & Eastenson, 1988; Nelson & Aboud, 1985). Their views of what constitutes a moral transgression toward another child differs notably in the two relationships, even as preschoolers (Slomkowski & Killen, in press). They can be considerably more forgiving of friends. And one study reports that 4-year-olds who were termed "good friends" more frequently solved a Prisoner's Dilemma game with moral sensitivity than did friends who were less close (Matsumoto, Haan, Yabrove, Theodorou, & Carney, 1986). The moral sensibility of young children concerning their friends is indeed often in marked contrast to their moral position as regards their siblings! Consider the following replies from a 5-year-old from the Pennsylvania study, first in relation to questions about moral transgressions involving his sister and then in relation to his friend, Jeff:

> *Interviewer:* How about if your sister took a toy from you—would that be OK or not OK?
>
> *Child:* Not OK! I would be pissed off, and I would kick her!
>
> *Interviewer:* Why?
>
> *Child:* Because she'd be taking something from me. Because she'd be stealing it. A CRIME!
>
> *Interviewer:* What about if Jeff took something from you?
>
> *Child:* That would be OK . . . because I wouldn't mind.
>
> *Interviewer:* How about if you took a toy from Jeff?
>
> *Child:* I would never do it. Because he's my friend. My best, best, best, best friend!

> *Interviewer:* What about if you took a toy from your sister? Would that
> be OK or not OK?
> *Child:* OK . . . because she's my sister and I hate her guts. . . . Well, I
> don't actually hate her, but . . .

To do justice to the nature of friendships between young children, two issues must be acknowledged at the outset. The first is the importance of friendships to children. No parent or teacher can fail to notice not only the significance of friendships in young children's lives but also the loneliness and unhappiness of children without friends (Cassidy & Asher, 1992). Second, an exciting and distinctive world opens up for a child with the development of friendships, one that reflects a special understanding and skill on the part of the children. As Gottman and his colleagues note in the introduction to their book on children's friendships:

> Friends can create a world of great involvement and high adventure, and they can do it at the tender age of 3 or 4. They must coordinate their efforts with all the virtuosity of an accomplished jazz quartet, and they must manage the amount of conflict between them. These things require enormous social skill. (Gottman & Parker, 1986, p. 3)

Very young children do not articulate with any elaboration their understanding of friendship or what they value in their particular friendships. They are most likely to say simply, "We play together". This used to be taken as evidence against the importance or subtlety of their friendships. Yet as Gottman and his colleagues have shown, the establishment of a shared world of play is in itself an achievement that depends on a close meshing of interests, goals, and intellectual excitement—and that requires subduing one's own wishes in the interests of the joint play. As Parker and Gottman (1989) point out, basing conclusions about mutuality and stability of the relationship solely on self-report data from these young children does such friendships a disservice. Moreover, even when children have the verbal and cognitive skills to describe their relationships more elaborately, they are not—any more than adults—always aware of how they relate to their friends. Little correspondence is seen between children's reports of intimacy in their relationships and rates of self-disclosure in friendship interaction (Hobart, 1987) or between friends' expectations of prosocial behavior and their actual prosocial behavior (Berndt, 1986).

What do we know of individual differences in the quality of young children's friendships—their dimensions, origins, and implications? So far, most research on friendships has focused on delineating the differences between friendships and other peer relations; however, because the qualities of friendships vary widely among older individuals, and they probably will differ also among young children.

Dimensions of Difference

To begin to describe and assess friendships, we need methods that are sensitive to the reciprocity and intensity of mutual liking, that include the perceptions of children themselves, and that allow us to capture the dimensions central to friendship, such as coordinated play, shared fantasy, teasing, joking, and gossip. Investigators have now developed open-ended interviews with children (e.g., Berndt, Hawkins, & Hoyle, 1986; Berndt & Perry, 1986) and interviews and questionnaires that focus on children's own evaluations of their friendships (Bukowski, Hoza, & Newcomb, 1987; Furman & Buhrmester, 1985; Parker & Asher, 1990). For the early years of childhood, behavioral identification of friends, reciprocal nomination (e.g., Howes, 1987), and—probably the most revealing of all—observation or tape recording of friends without parents or observers present have been used (Gottman & Parker, 1986; Kramer, 1990; Slomkowski & Dunn, 1992). From these studies, what relationship qualities stand out as most important?

AFFECTION, ENJOYMENT, CARING, AND SUPPORT

Friends are important, children tell us, because of the pleasures and excitement of the joint play that happens with a friend; because of the companionship, the support, and the help they provide; and the affection that is felt in a friendship. The hallmarks of friendship are affection for the other and enjoyment of the other's company. When school-aged children are asked about their friendships, some studies report close links between individual differences in the various positive features of the relationship: companionship, prosocial actions, intimacy, loyalty, and attachment were found by Berndt and Perry (1986) to be closely linked at Grades 2, 4, and 6, for instance. Others find that among 6- to 7-year-olds, companionship on the one hand and intimacy and caring on the other are relatively separate dimensions (Stocker & Mantz-Simmons, in press). More work is obviously needed on the nature of friendship dimensions in young children; however, what is already clear is that wide individual differences are found between friend pairs in each of these positive aspects of the relationship from the preschool period through middle childhood. Children in middle childhood vary considerably, for example, in the extent to which they report feeling affection for their friends, and they also vary considerably in how much they express positive excitement and happiness when they are together.

Children also vary in the extent to which they express concern for and try to see how they could help and support their friends. Even very young friends can show considerable concern and make practical efforts to find ways of comforting their friends. Blum (1987) discusses the significance of these early signs of concern in the context of examples that include the following incident involving 3-year-old Sarah: "Sarah, three, gives Clara, three, her own Donald Duck hat (to keep 'forever'), saying that she has done so because Clara has (recently, but not in the moment) lost her (Boston) Celtics cap" (Blum, 1987, p. 310).

Blum points out that in this and other examples that Sarah "responds not to an immediate state of distress of the other child but draws on her memory and knowledge of the other child's condition. . . . Sarah's responsiveness is not to a specific state of distress but rather simply to what she believes Clara wants or would like." He notes further that this "responsiveness" involves the "taking of action to address another's condition. It thus involves a kind of initiative and is not merely a passive response to another person" (Blum, 1987, p. 311). As the example we quoted above shows, our interviews with the Pennsylvania children about moral issues made clear that some children's moral sensibility was heightened when they were considering moral breaches that involved their friends. Consider 5-year-old Eleanor, who answers questions about situations in which her friend was a victim of her own actions:

> *Interviewer:* What about if you wouldn't let Emily (her friend) play a game with you—would that be OK or not OK?
> *Eleanor:* Not OK! Because she'd wonder why I wouldn't let her play.
> *Interviewer:* How about if you called her a name?
> *Eleanor:* Not OK. Because it would hurt her feelings. Because I know all the F words and everything!

To the same questions concerning her brother, Eleanor simply said it would be all right for her to carry out such actions "Because he's a little brat . . . a fat brat!" (In fact, he was 5 years older than her!)

For the preschool and early childhood periods, we still know relatively little about how commonly young friends feel intense and long-lasting affection for one another. Sullivan (1953) held that the intimate and affectionate aspect of friendship did not appear until middle childhood. Yet clearly some young friends feel very close indeed to one another, separation from friends can cause distress, and friends can act as supports in times of change. Thus, children who made daycare transitions with their friends did better than those who lost their friends as a result of a daycare transition (Howes, 1987), and children who lost their friends because the friends moved away showed a decline in the frequency of competent social play with their peers over the subsequent year. These results echo the findings of another study showing that preschoolers whose friends moved away showed nontrivial signs of distress and anxiety (Field, 1984). In a study of children's perceptions and memories of their own daycare transitions, we found that 4- and 5-year-olds recalling their experiences 1 to 2 years earlier frequently cited their friends as the key to making them feel happy about the new daycare setting (Dunn, in press). The supportive role that friends can play for 3-year-old children undergoing the family upheaval of a sibling birth also has been demonstrated (Kramer, 1990).

Most notably, we know that children who grow up without appropriate "parental" attachment figures can develop extraordinarily supportive relationships with one another. The classic studies by Anna Freud and her colleagues of children who grew up in concentration camps and the description of the relations between the children in the Hampstead Nursery in World War II vividly reveal the support provided by the children for one another (Burlingham & Freud, 1944). And the classic studies by Harlow and his colleagues of young rhesus monkeys established the significance of supportive relationships between monkey peers for the adjustment of those growing up without parents.

We know little about how differences in this supportive aspect of friendship are linked to other features of how children actually behave toward their friends, although the interview studies suggest they may be closely associated with the other positive features of the relationship. By the school years, children who are less accepted by their peers tend to have more problems in their friendships, with less caring, help, and guidance than the friendships of well-accepted children (Parker & Asher, 1990).

Perhaps most striking of all in the relations between young friends is the significance of their joint play and companionship, as well as differences in the extent to which they play and communicate in a connected or coordinated way. Of interest is that the observational data in the Pennsylvania Sibling Study showed that the dimension of expressed positive affect between friends was relatively independent of the extent to which they sustained connected communication and play, and it also was independent of the dimension of shared fantasy in which the children engaged together (Slomkowski & Dunn, 1992).

CONNECTEDNESS AND COORDINATION OF PLAY

To coordinate play with a friend, a child must communicate clearly, attend to the perspective of the other, agree more than disagree, delay getting what she herself wants, and manage disagreements so that they do not lead to explosions and can be settled reasonably amicably. Connectedness of communication between children turns out to be key in whether they will progress toward friendship (Parker, 1986). Not surprisingly, children differ markedly in the extent to which they communicate in a connected way in particular friendships. In our Pennsylvania study, for instance, the conversations of 47-month-old children playing with their close friends (audiotaped without an observer present) revealed a wide range for the 50 friend dyads. The proportion of children's conversational turns that were part of connected communication ranged from 19% to 100% of conversational turns among the dyads, while the length of episodes of connected conversation ranged from 5 to 39 conversational turns per hour. A note of caution here: Measures of "connectedness" in young children are usually heavily dependent on verbal measures. We have not yet made much progress in assessing closeness between young friends when it is expressed nonverbally. As Howe and her colleagues wrote when discussing their observations of joint pretend play (Howes, Unger, & Matheson, 1992, p. 138):

> We find it relatively easy to judge connectedness to others when two girls tenderly cooperate in putting the babies to bed and very difficult to judge connectiveness to others when two boys spend fifteen minutes in harmonious and violent motorcycle racing. We have not discovered how to ask these 5-year-old motorcycle racers to explain how or if the play deepens their friendship.

SHARED FANTASY

One feature stands out as of special significance in some friendships. The excitement of many best-friend relationships in early childhood lies in the shared fantasies that the children develop together. Gottman sees joint fantasy play as "the highest level of coordinated play," with its demands of involvement that requires the "willingness to go on an adventure with someone else, to influence and to accept influence." The ratio of individuals' agreement to disagreement with their partners is higher during episodes of joint fantasy than in any other communicative exchange (Gottman, 1986). The individual differences between friend pairs in the extent to which they engage in shared fantasy are quite marked: Among our Pennsylvanian 4-year-olds, the range was from 0 to 78% of their conversational turns during joint play (the mean number of turns in 1 hour was 28 turns, *SD* 24). Many different functions have been attributed to this shared pretend play, and a convincing case has been made for shared fantasy as a context in which children begin to explore intimacy, trust, and self-disclosure (Howes et al., 1992).

SHARED HUMOR, GOSSIP, AND SELF-DISCLOSURE

Just as sibling pairs differ in the part that shared humor plays in their relationship, so too the relationships between friends vary considerably in the extent of shared humor the children enjoy. Some friends giggle together over a continuing stream of jokes, while for others such joking together is rare. In our Pennsylvania study, some common themes of the jokes that the 5-year-olds shared stood out. Gender was one: The comment, "Hey, now I look like a guy!" from one girl as she put on a false moustache brought both 5-year-olds to helpless giggles. Jokes about underpants, diapers, and toilets also were very common: Pretending that toy figures "forgot their underpants! They all need to go potty!" was a common source of joint laughter; so, too, were jokes about one's own inadequacy or mistakes. When one child asked her friend, "Why did you do that?" the reply, "I don't know why I did—that's a problem!" brought them to laugh together. Word play along scatological lines was also a source of amusement, as in the following exchange between two 5-year-olds were playing side by side with a construction kit.

Child (dropping something): Whoopadoopa!
Friend: Poopadoopa! You're a poopadoopa!

Catherine Garvey's (1977, 1984) studies have documented the variation on rhymes, intonation, and word shape that children's jokes with friends often include. The next example is a small piece of a long exchange between a 5-year-old boy and a 5-year-old girl, who knew each other well, in her study; they took seven consecutive turns playing on the phrase "grandmother, grandmomma," before the exchange continued thus:

> *Girl:* Momma I . . . my mommy momma. Mother Humpf.
> *Boy:* Hey.
> *Girl:* Mother mear. (Laughs.) Mother smear.
> *Boy:* (Laughs.)
> *Girl:* I said mother smear mother near mother tear mother dear. (Laughs.)
> *Boy:* Peer.
> *Girl:* Fear.
> *Boy:* Pooper.
> *Girl:* What?
> *Boy:* Pooper. Now that's a . . . that's a good name. (Garvey, 1977, pp. 70-71)

In the interchange, as Garvey notes, "the stress and pitch possibilities and the common lexical variations were fairly well exhausted by this pair." With these exchanges we witness the shared pleasure in playing with words that is rarely seen between children and their parents. It is a special feature of children's relationships with familiar friends and with affectionate siblings.

Gossip and self-disclosure also are important features of friendship. Even among friends who are as young as 3 or 4 years of age, gossip begins to surface as a salient dimension. Frequently, these early gossip exchanges are comments about other children with a strong negative, critical, or derisory tone, and they typically include references to "we." Here are a 4-year-old and a 5-year-old from Gottman's (1986) study:

> *B:* Danny and Jeff did that. They did. They're dumb, aren't they?
> *S:* Yeah.
> *B:* Aren't they?
> *S:* Yeah.

And in another exchange:

> *S:* Go! We want her to go away.
> *B:* We don't want Allison here to bother us again.

S: We're very mad at her.
B: We are very mad. (Gottman, 1986, pp. 166-167)

Typically, young friends join forces in agreeing that "we" are different from whoever is the target of gossip, and such exchanges reinforce solidarity between the friends. Often a gossiping comment about another child is followed by both friends making self-disclosing comments, reinforcing the "me, too" atmosphere. Here are two 5-year-old boys from the Pennsylvania study discussing a child in their class at school:

Child: Remember old Wilbur at school? Remember him? I hate him, do you?
Friend: I hate him, don't you?
Child: Yes, everybody hates him at school.
Friend: Well, Wilbur loves me, and I hate him!

The detailed studies of young children's friendships carried out by Howes and her colleagues showed that 4-year-old friends engaged in more self-disclosure than did other children who were friends and that pairs of children who had been friends for a long period were more likely to self-disclose than were "contemporary" friends (Howes et al., 1992).

Although many preschool-aged friends do not gossip at any length or make frequent self-disclosing comments, by middle childhood successful negative-evaluation gossip is responded to with great interest, with yet more gossiping comments, and an encouraging sense of solidarity between friends. It forms the core of many middle childhood friendships (Gottman & Mettetal, 1986). The extent to which young friends talk about secrets, problems, or fears also varies considerably. A greater range of individual differences is found here than in the other, more positive aspects of the relationship (Dunn & Beardsall, in preparation; Stocker, personal communication), and some gender differences are suggested, with girls more likely to share secrets and problems with their friends than were boys. Some children never talk about their secret problems or fears with their friends, while others do so often and value this theme in their friendships.

CONFLICT, COMPETITIVENESS, AND CONTROL

The relation of conflict, competitiveness, and jealousy to other dimensions of friendship is not yet clear. When young children are interviewed, their answers frequently suggest that they think that friends do not quarrel and that sharing and helping are incompatible with conflict. But observational work clearly shows that friends do argue and quarrel and are competitive with one another; indeed, competitiveness between young male friends may be more frequent than among male acquaintances (Hartup, 1989). Other research indicates that individual differences in the hostile aspects of the relationship are less marked than in the friendly dimensions and that less variability is seen in conflict and competitiveness between friends than is found in emotional support (and less variability is found than in the conflict between siblings). Differences in how children resolve their conflicts with friends, however, are quite marked among the 4- and 5-year-olds in our Pennsylvania study (Slomkowski & Dunn, 1992). Observational research also reveals individual differences between friend pairs in the balance of control in the relationship. Although friendship theoretically is the reciprocal relationship par excellence, in some friendships one child dominates, controls, and gets his way, while more equity is found in others.

Developmental Changes

Studies of how friendship changes in nature as children grow up have focused chiefly on normative developments. Intimacy, self-disclosure, and emotional support become more prominent features of the relationship as children grow through middle childhood toward adolescence (Berndt & Ladd, 1989). We do not know what this means for patterns of individual differences in friendship over time. For children whose individual characteristics make them particularly open to intimacy and self-disclosure, the possibilities for close friendship may increase as they reach adolescence. Also, a child who makes friends easily in early childhood is not necessarily a "natural" for close relationships in adolescence. We simply do not yet have the longitudinal information to answer these questions.

The wider social context also probably affects children's close friendships in a variety of ways. For example, life events that influence children's family relationships also may well affect their friendships. We know that changes in preschool or daycare arrangements have considerable impact when children lose touch with their friends (Field, 1984). Clearly, changing schools in the early and middle childhood years is likely to affect children's friendships in the short term, as is the experience of moving into a new house or changing neighborhoods.

Individual Differences in Children and the Quality of Friendship

Because studies of young children's friendships are still rather few, we know relatively little about how individual differences in children's characteristics affect their relationships with their close friends in the preschool and early childhood years. Different aspects of temperament and cognitive ability probably affect different dimensions of friendships. Thus, for instance, we found in the Pennsylvania study that children's temperamental characteristics were related to the connectedness of their relationship with their friends. Children who were high on the temperamental trait of sociability at 33 months engaged in more connected play with their friends at 47 months than did other children, while individual differences in whether children reasoned and attempted to resolve conflict through argument or simply reasserted their own position were linked to differences in the temperamental trait of activity. Children who were rated as very active at 33 months were less likely to resolve conflicts with reasoned argument, and they also were less connected in their relationships with their friends at 47 months than the rest of the sample (Slomkowski & Dunn, 1992). Ideally, we would have information on the temperamental characteristics of both children in a friendship to assess the impact of temperament on their relationship. Just as we saw that the temperament match of both children in the sibling relationship was important for the quality of their relationship, so too the personalities of both children in a friendship pair is likely to be important in their relationship. The temperamental "match" may be closer for friends than it is for siblings, because friends, after all, can choose each other, whereas siblings must spend time together in great intimacy without any choice.

The same point—that we need information on both children in a friendship pair to understand the contribution of individual differences to the relationship qualities—applies to the question of whether individual children's emotional adjustment, such as their propensity toward internalizing or externalizing problems, contributes to the quality of their friendship. By the time children reach middle childhood and early adolescence, some links between differences in adjustment and friendship quality are evident. For the children in the Cambridge study, for instance, differences in internalizing and externalizing problems were related to the kind of friendship they described with a close friend. The 10-year-old secondborn siblings who scored high on externalizing problems on the Child Behavior Checklist (Achenbach & Edelbrock, 1983) were more likely to report hostility and fighting with their close friends [$r(40)= .35$] than were the rest of the sample. On the other hand, their adolescent older siblings, those who scored high on internalizing problems, reported less overt hostility and negativity in their friendships [$r(40)= -.31$]. The links between quality of friendship and adjustment become strong during middle childhood and early adolescence (Berndt & Perry, 1990); troubled children have more difficulty maintaining friendships (Hartup, 1986), and those referred to guidance clinics have fewer and less stable friendships (Selman, 1980). Again, the direction of effects in these examples is not clear; causal influence probably goes both ways. One longitudinal study reports, for instance, an association between emotional disorder in school-aged children and the presence of moderate to poor friendships in the 12 months preceding the onset of the disorder (Goodyer, Wright, & Altham, 1989).

Gender also may play a part in contributing to differences in qualities of young children's close friendships. Some evidence in our Cambridge sample suggests that, by middle childhood, girls are more likely than boys to share secrets with their friends and to discuss problems and feelings (Dunn & Beardsall, in preparation), and the Pennsylvanian study indicates that gender differences in talk about feelings and self-disclosure with friends are evident even among the 5-year-olds. Several studies have suggested that intimacy is more central to the friendships of girls than boys in middle childhood and adolescence, a finding replicated in some but not all studies (Berndt & Perry, 1990). As Berndt and Perry point out, we do not yet know whether boys lag behind girls in developing intimate friendships or never develop friendships that are on average as intimate as girls' friendships. In any case, individual differences in intimacy in friendship—our concern here— are marked for both boys and girls.

Most prominent in discussions of the contribution of individual differences to peer relations is the idea that differences in children's social understanding explain differences in their peer relationships (Berndt & Ladd, 1989). Although very little information is available on friendships (as opposed to peer popularity) in this regard, we note with interest that in the Pennsylvania study children who performed very successfully on the assessments of social understanding as 40-month-olds were particularly likely to share extended, elaborate fantasy with their friends and to enjoy especially long "connected communication" with their close friends (Slomkowski & Dunn, submitted, a). Of course, such correlational links tell us nothing about cause or about the direction of effects. Although children who are skilled at understanding what another child is feeling may be especially good at sharing and developing a joint pretend narrative, the experience of such play also may foster this understanding. Indeed, both processes probably are happening. We should, however, be careful about jumping to the conclusion that differences in friendship quality can be explained largely in terms of an individual's social skills or understanding. As we will see in the later chapters, some evidence does not support such a story. It is widely suggested, however, that such individual differences in social understanding are importantly influenced by the parent-child relationship. This point brings us to the topic of the next two chapters: What are the connections between these different relationships?

Connections Between Relationships Within the Family

Differences between children in the qualities of each of their relationships are striking. A key developmental question raised by these differences in parent-and-child, sibling, or close friends' relationships is whether systematic links can be found among them. Do children's relationships with their mothers, for instance, serve as a template for their other relationships? This idea has wide currency today, and so too has the idea that how a parent was "mothered" will influence his or her own parental behavior. Are differences in the quality of parent-child relationships systematically related to differences in the relationships between their parents, or between children and their siblings? Family systems theorists' views are now frequently considered by psychologists and are beginning to be explored empirically (see, for example, Gable, Belsky, & Crnic, in press; Hinde & Stevenson-Hinde, 1988; Kaye & Furstenberg, 1985; Kreppner & Lerner, 1989). What about links between children's relationships with their siblings, parents, and friends? Do children who have affectionate, cooperative relationships with their siblings, for instance, develop friendships with their peers more easily than those who have more conflicted sibling relationships? In this and the next chapter we look at ideas concerning the links between relationships and evidence for those links—both concurrent and over time.

Before this evidence is considered, we should recognize three general issues that are central to any attempt to answer questions about connections between relationships. The most difficult of these is the issue of *what* processes might mediate the links between relationships. Does the child develop some sort of model or expectation for relationships within one relationship that influences the nature of his or her later relationships—the idea that currently is of much interest to attachment theorists? Could it be that the confidence, self-concept, or self-esteem of an individual is affected by an early relationship, and this then influences or constrains the nature of the relationships he or she forms later in life? Is the quality of both early and late relationships affected by some common causal factor—such as the personality of the individual or the stress under which he or she is living? All of these processes might be important; the challenge is to document which are salient for which children and at which stages of development.

This question of what mechanisms underlie the links between relationships is notoriously intractable. The kind of answer that people find for it will be much affected by the nature of the theoretical perspective from which they study relationships. This brings us to a second general issue: The inferences made about the processes that link relationships will be deeply influenced by the way in which those relationships are described: by the level of abstraction, generality, and diversity of the dimensions chosen and by the assumptions made about which dimensions are most significant. Our theoretical backgrounds will inevitably influence the assumptions we make about what matters within a relationship, and thus they will affect the dimensions we choose to describe it and the consequent account we give of how this relationship may be linked to others. If, for example, we think that cognitive attributional processes are of significance in the influence of relationships upon relationships, then we will include measures of such features of interaction in our description of relationships and thus make it possible to confirm or disconfirm our hypotheses. If, however, our view is that broad emotional aspects of relationships are key, then we might well not include such measures in our initial descriptive base—and we would then, of course, not find a role for such cognitive processes in the pattern of links between relationships.

A third general issue concerns developmental change. Just as the dimensions that characterize relationships change with children's development, so too the processes that link relationships may well change as children grow up. Each issue should be borne in mind in considering the following brief summary of evidence on connections between relationships. We begin at a descriptive level with the question, What associations are there between differences in marital relationships and parent-child relationships?

Marital and Parent-Child Relationships

Are differences in parent-child relationships influenced by the relationships that parents have with their own spouses (as we might expect in Hinde's model)? A common assumption is that these relationships are closely interconnected (Minuchin, 1985), especially given the evidence that poor marital relationships are associated with poor child outcome (Gable et al., in press). However, the nature, direction, and mechanisms underlying the associations between the relationships are not as clear as might be supposed. Most research supports the idea that good marital relationships are associated with good parent-child relationships, while difficulties in parent-child relations are more common in families with poor marriages. For example, studies of the transition to parenthood show that mothers' expressed affection for their babies and their competence are associated with the quality of their marriages (Easterbrooks & Emde, 1988). Security of attachment between mother and child is reported to be more common in families that have warm, supportive marital relationships (Belsky, 1984; Goldberg & Easterbrooks, 1984), and more generally the quality of mother-child relationships is reported to be less adequate in families having marital conflict or lacking support from one spouse (e.g., Christensen & Margolin, 1988; Engfer, 1988;

Quinton & Rutter, 1988; Rutter, 1988). Hostility between spouses is reported to be related to less effective or authoritarian parenting (e.g., de Brock & Vermulst, 1991; Stoneman, Brody, & Burke, 1989). Conflict between mother and child in laboratory settings is reported to be negatively correlated with the quality of the marriage (Meyer, 1988), while fathers who feel their marriage is happy describe themselves as warmer and less aggravated by their children than do other men (Easterbrooks & Emde, 1988).

Note, however, that in families not under social or psychological stress, the links between marital and parent-child relationships are not as clear-cut or consistent as those in studies of distressed families. In the study by Goldberg and Easterbrooks, for instance, security of child-parent attachment was not associated with marital adjustment for the "middle range" of marital quality. Moving away from global indices of marital quality and toward more precise and specific measures of different dimensions of marital relationships may well be important if we are to explore the possible associations with parent-child relationships, as McHale and her colleagues have argued (McHale, Freitag, Crouter, & Bartko, 1991). Some evidence supports the idea that "compensatory" processes also can be important: A stressed or unsatisfactory marriage can lead to a parent seeking to satisfy a need for love within his or her relationship with a child (Brody, Pillegrini, & Sigel, 1986; Engfer, 1988; Goth-Owens, Stollak, Messe, Peshkess, & Watts, 1982). And, of course, for families under stress, poor marital and difficult parent-child relationships may both be the consequence of other stresses, rather than be linked directly.

The complexity of these findings suggests several general lessons. First, the connections between marital and parent-child relationships may be different for fathers and mothers (Brody et al., 1986; Easterbrooks & Emde, 1988; Gable et al., in press) and for sons and daughters (Hetherington, 1988). Indeed, the marriage may well have more influence on father-child relationships than on mother-child relationships (Belsky, 1990). Second, the associations may depend on the degree of stress on the marital relationship (Goldberg & Easterbrooks, 1984). And third, the connections may differ according to the particular indices of the marital and parent-child relationships that are chosen. Indeed, all of the studies considered in a recent review reported inconsistencies in this last respect (Dunn, 1988b). The importance of moving away from global characterizations of relationships is again highlighted.

Finally, we note one promising new direction of research on the links between parent-child and marital relationships: the focus on the significance of the "coparenting" alliance—the extent to which mothers and fathers support or undermine each other in dealing with their children (Floyd & Zmich, 1991; Weissman & Cohen, 1985). The marital and coparenting relationships apparently are related in some ways and yet are also distinctive in their association with parent-child relationships (Gable et al., in press).

PROCESSES IMPLICATED

Several explanations for these connections between marital and parent-child relationships can be offered. The association between a good marital relationship and a harmonious parent-child relationship could lie in some attribute of the parents that led both of them to choose a supportive spouse and develop a good marriage and thus to a good parent-child relationship. Genetics might well play a part in such a link, given the evidence for genetic influence on personality and on aspects of the parent-child relationship such as warmth (Plomin & Bergeman, 1991).

Another idea is that a good marriage may enhance a woman's well-being and sense of self-esteem or of being valued; this in turn affects her relations with her child. Note that the direction of causal processes could run in either direction here and in the other processes discussed. Some versions of this idea propose a direct carry-over from the emotional quality of one relationship to another: The affection expressed and experienced in one relationship, for example, carries over to the other relationship. Other versions are that a good marriage affects a parent not through its relationship quality but in a more general way as one aspect of the parent's environment. Other suggestions are that marital support affects the parent-child relationship through instrumental help with the demands and tasks of parenting. Rutter (1988) and his colleagues' study of women who had been reared as children in institutions provides some clarifying information here. The analyses showed that although choice of spouse was linked to some aspects of the girls' earlier personality and functioning (such as a propensity to plan), the effects of marital support were stronger and held after controlling for these "planning" effects. Moreover, the functioning of the men before they met the women was also linked to the latter's later parenting, suggesting that we should not attribute the effects of marital support only to the influence of wife on spouse: Both adults probably influenced each other.

A variety of sources also provide evidence that supports the hypothesis that a good spousal relationship affects the parent-child relationship through rather broad effects on a parent's life (and presumably also a child's life), not solely through "relationship" effects. For instance, the protective effects of marital support are evident in a wide range of aspects of functioning aside from parenting, while a variety of stresses other than a poor spousal relationship are associated with difficulties in parent-child relationships, such as, for example, poor socioeconomic and housing circumstances. Rutter has argued that we need to consider separately the effects of lack of support versus support from the effects of the stress of a poor marital relationship; he points out that this same point is evident when we examine the protective effect on parent-child relationships of parents' supportive relationships outside the family. Thus, evidence suggests that supportive, confiding relationships with adults can mitigate the effects of stressful life events on parents; furthermore, the lack of such relationships can increase the adverse consequences of such stress (Brown & Harris, 1978).

The supportive effects of relationships beyond the family are evident not only for disadvantaged families, but also more generally, as Crockenberg (1981) demonstrated in her study of mother-child pairs, half of whom were middle-class. The social support received by young mothers was the best predictor of the security of their children's attachment to them. Such supportive relationships are likely to be of special significance to mother-child pairs who are living under stress.

Continuities Across Generations

Differences in parent-child relationships, then, are associated with the quality of the parent's spousal relationship, as well as with the presence or absence of other supportive relationships for parents. What about the widely held view that these differences in parent-child relationships are also affected by the parent's own childhood experience of being parented? At one extreme—the case of child abuse—associations are indeed reported between the experience of being abused by a parent and later inadequate parenting and difficult parent-child relationships (Belsky, 1978; Kaufman & Zigler, 1986). Within the more normal range of differences in parent-child relationships, the most illuminating strategy used to investigate this question has been prospective longitudinal research that follows individuals from their own childhood to adulthood and parenthood. Two notable studies of this sort both report considerable intergenerational continuities in parent-child relationships.

The first study, by Rutter and his colleagues (see above), was of women reared in institutions. When these 89 women were studied as parents with 2-year-old children, the results showed that difficult parent-child relationships were much more common than in the control group of mothers who were from the same neighborhood but had grown up in families (40% as compared to 11% with difficulties). Note that although nearly one third of the 89 women had good relationships with their children, the evidence for associations between institutional upbringing and poor parent-child relationships was strong. The difficulties the women had in their relationships with their 2-year-olds could have arisen from a variety of factors: The women had suffered a broad range of adversities. But one of the most important predictors was whether they had suffered serious breakdowns in their relationships with their own parents before they were 4 years old.

The second study is the follow-up by Elder and his colleagues of individuals who participated in the Berkeley Growth Study (Caspi & Elder, 1988; Elder, 1979). Here the investigators show how growing up in a family in which the parent-child relationship was hostile and unaffectionate was associated with the development of personal instabilities; these instabilities were seen in (1) the tension of the second generation's marital relationship and (2) erratic discipline and conflict in their relationships with their own children. These third-generation children were likely to develop problems; they were described by their own children as bad-tempered, and their own husbands described them also as explosive in their relations with their own fourth-generation children.

Of course, we face serious difficulties in drawing clear conclusions about the processes that might mediate these links across generations. First, the links might reflect genetic influences rather than the effects of early experience. In many cases, the girls in Rutter's study were institutionalized because their own parents were persistent criminals or suffered from major psychiatric disorders. When this parental deviance was taken into account (as a proxy for genetic risk), however, a strong effect of disrupted parenting persisted.

Second, for many of the women in the institution study, the adverse experiences of infancy continued through childhood, adolescence, and adulthood. We cannot then assume that the problematic parent-child relationships were solely the result of the women's own childhood experiences. Rather, we now recognize that many indirect effects may lead to chains of experiences between a disrupted childhood and a poor marriage and difficult parent-child relationship—connections "between experiences so that one bad (or good) experience makes another one more likely" (Rutter, 1991).

Making inferences about the nature of connections between relationships across generations is even more problematic with retrospective research. Recent years have seen a vogue for such research within an attachment paradigm. Mothers of "securely" and "insecurely" attached children are asked to recall their own childhood experiences, and the results indicate that those whose children are securely attached describe more acceptance and less rejection from their own mothers than do women with insecurely attached children (e.g., Ricks, 1985); they also identify positively with their own mothers, recall them as nurturant (Morris, 1980,

1981), have rich memories of their childhood attachment relationships (Grossman, Fremmer-Brombik, Rudolph, & Grossman, 1988), and recall their own attachment history with coherence and readiness (Main, Kaplan, & Cassidy, 1985). Clearly, these differences in perceptions of childhood are important and interesting, but these happy memories may be strongly influenced by the women's current circumstances. We could not conclude from these data alone that their earlier relationships were indeed different from those of the mothers of insecurely attached children, and we certainly could not conclude that a causal link could be found between the two relationships. Having an easy relationship with a securely attached child may well contribute to a woman's rosy view of life, including her perspective on her own childhood. Fitting with such an interpretation is the evidence that women who reported having had bad experiences in childhood, but who had come to terms with these experiences, also had securely attached children (Grossman et al., 1988). Again the question of what mechanisms underlie such connections remains an intractable one. The possibility that genetic influence mediates the association in part remains to be tested, as does the possibility that continuity in personality contributes to the connection.

Parent-Child and Parent-Sibling Relationships

If we focus on the parent-child relationships of siblings within the same family, we learn three important lessons. First, the siblings' relationships with the "shared" parents differ—in some cases, markedly so; second, children are very sensitive to such differences; and third, these differences appear to have considerable developmental impact on the children over time.

Evidence for the differences in siblings' relationships with their parents comes from a variety of sources: From observations of family interaction in both structured videotaped settings and more naturalistic unstructured observations, from interviews with children, and from interviews with parents themselves (see Dunn & Plomin, 1990, for a review). For instance, in spite of strong social expectations that all children within a family should be loved equally, only one third of the parents in the Colorado Sibling Study reported feeling a similar intensity of affection for both their children when the children were on average 4 and 7 years old. Differences also were noted in the attention and disciplinary exchanges in the two relationships. For instance, only 12% of parents reported that disciplinary exchanges were equally frequent with both children, and only one third said they gave similar attention to both. Observations of mothers at home with their children—whether from the videotaped settings of the Colorado study or the naturalistic observations of families in Cambridge—confirmed that, at any one time, mothers behaved differently with their two children.

We can hardly be surprised, of course, that parents looking after both a preschooler or toddler and a relatively sophisticated 5- to 8-year-old behave differently toward their two children, given the differences in the children's developmental stage. Indeed, the Colorado study showed us that children's particular developmental stage was strongly related to individual differences in their mothers' interaction with them. As we described in chapter 2, the results showed that a mother who was relatively affectionate to her first child at 12 months of age also was affectionate to her second child as a 12-month-old—relative to the other mothers; however, she was not particularly affectionate to the same child over time. Some mothers were especially affectionate toward their children as 1-year-olds; others particularly enjoyed 2-year-olds or the more talkative 3-year-olds.

The key implication of these findings is that at any one time, when the siblings are at different ages and developmental stages, their mothers will be behaving very differently toward them. For instance, in a family in which the mother delights especially in her 1-year-old but finds an argumentative 2½-year-old more trying, the latter child will daily witness the special affection the mother feels for her baby. The second point underlined by studies of siblings' relationships with their parents is that, from a remarkably early age, children are extremely sensitive witnesses to any such differences in parental affection, interest, and discipline. This sensitivity is shown both in their comments about the pattern of family relationships and in the way they react to interactions between their parents and siblings.

Children's comments about differences in parental treatment are vivid and make the salience of such relative differences clear—especially if the children are firstborn. The 5- and 6-year-olds in Helen Koch's (1960) classic study perceived plenty of inequities: "She gets more attention." "People are on her side." They also often saw themselves as favored in some ways: "If I cry for things, mother says let me have them." "I can hit her but she can't hit me." "I can do dangerous things that my brother can't do." "I don't have to eat spinach."

The studies of children's reactions to interaction between parent and sibling confirm the salience of this parent-sibling relationship for children from the end of the first year onward. Two studies in Cambridge show that both firstborn and laterborn children reacted very promptly to a high proportion (as many as 3 of 4) of the interactions between their mothers and siblings (Dunn & Munn, 1985; Kendrick & Dunn, 1983). They were especially attentive to interactions in which emotions were expressed, whether disputes, playful games, or affectionate cuddles. And studies of their conversations showed that they monitored closely the talk between their mothers and siblings and interrupted such conversations to draw attention to themselves with growing effectiveness during the third year (Dunn & Shatz, 1989).

So, parents behave differently with their various children, and children are very sensitive to such differences. What gives these two points their developmental significance is that these differences in siblings' experiences with their parents are linked to outcome differences in the children. For example, the emotional adjustment of the firstborn children in the Colorado sample was linked to their experience of differential maternal treatment. Children's worrying, anxiety, and depression was associated with differential maternal affection or control; those children who experienced less affection or more control than their siblings were more likely to be anxious or depressed (Dunn, Stocker, & Plomin, 1990). Of course, no inferences can be made about the causal direction of such a link: Mothers could well be responding with less affection to children who are anxious or depressed than to their more outgoing and happy children. Children's antisocial behavior (disobedience, teasing, and argumentativeness) was also linked to differential experiences with their mothers. Children were more likely to show high levels of such behavior in families in which mothers controlled them more than they controlled siblings. Again, we cannot draw conclusions about the direction of effects here. These differences in parent-child relationships for siblings in the same family are part of the "nonshared" experiences that behavior geneticists have shown to be important in explaining the development of individual differences in personality and adjustment.

A second example comes from the study of a national sample of adolescent siblings (Daniels, Dunn, Furstenberg, & Plomin, 1985). Here, both parental and sibling reports indicated that the sibling who had been closest to the mother, had more say in family decision making, and had higher parental chore expectations as compared to his or her siblings was better adjusted psychologically. And as a third example, in our Cambridge study we examined the self-esteem of the siblings when they were on average 6 and 9 years of age and found that the marked differences in the siblings' perceived self-competence were related to differential maternal and paternal behavior, both at the time that the children were assessed and at earlier periods. This link between parental differential treatment and the children's perceived self-competence was independent of earlier differences in the children's temperamental characteristics. Children whose mothers had shown relatively more affection to their siblings had lower senses of self-competence and self-worth than did children whose mothers had shown them relatively more affection than their siblings.

The message of these findings is that we need to consider the significance of children's relationships with their parents not as a dyad isolated from the other relationships within the family, but especially in relation to that parent's relationships with the other children in the family. Apparently, what matters developmentally is not only how loved or attended to by the mother or father a child feels, but also how loved or attended to he feels compared with his siblings. The processes of monitoring, protest, and social comparison that appear to be implicated in these links between child-parent and sibling-parent relationships are, it seems, operating very early in siblings' lives. As we will see in the next section, a close look at the trio of parent, child, and sibling in early childhood can be particularly revealing.

Parent-Child and Sibling-Child Relationships

If we consider the evidence for links between parent-child and child-sibling relationships, a principle central to understanding the links between different relationships quickly becomes apparent: Many different processes are probably involved in these connections. A close look at the trio of relationships between a mother and her two young children not only shows us the complexity of interconnections among the three relationships, but also highlights several quite different mechanisms that may link them. The findings of our studies in Cambridge and the United States showed that these range from general emotional disturbance as a mediating link to processes of increasing specificity and cognitive complexity. In other words, they range from processes involving general effects on relationship qualities to processes in which one specific relationship is connected with another.

First, consider the relationship of firstborn children and their mothers before and immediately following the birth of a sibling and the relationship that develops between the two siblings in the ensuing year. The arrival of a new sibling is accompanied by sharp changes in the relationship between mother and firstborn, and some children respond to these changes and the events surrounding the birth with considerable emotional disturbance (Dunn & Kendrick, 1982; Gottlieb & Mendelson, 1990; Stewart, Mobley, Van Tuyl, & Salvador, 1987; Vandell, 1987). For example, some children reacted in our Cambridge study with extreme withdrawal, and their relations with their mothers suffered a sharp drop in communicative interaction; these children were especially hostile to their younger siblings 1 year later, and their siblings were very

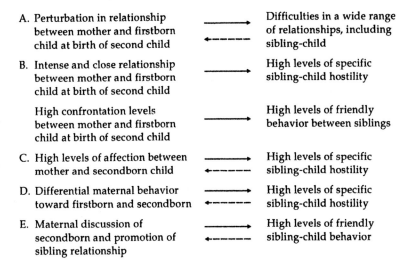

A. Perturbation in relationship between mother and firstborn child at birth of second child → Difficulties in a wide range of relationships, including sibling-child

B. Intense and close relationship between mother and firstborn child at birth of second child → High levels of specific sibling-child hostility

High confrontation levels between mother and firstborn child at birth of second child → High levels of friendly behavior between siblings

C. High levels of affection between mother and secondborn child → High levels of specific sibling-child hostility

D. Differential maternal behavior toward firstborn and secondborn → High levels of specific sibling-child hostility

E. Maternal discussion of secondborn and promotion of sibling relationship → High levels of friendly sibling-child behavior

Figure 5.1. Connections Between Mother-Child and Sibling Relationships.

negative to them (Dunn & Kendrick, 1982). One interpretation of these findings is that (1) the experience of changes that accompanied the sibling birth led to a general emotional disturbance for some children, and (2) this general disturbance colored much of the children's social behavior and relationships, including their relationships with their siblings. The process that links a mother-child relationship and a sibling-child relationship, according to this view, is a connection mediated by the child's general emotional well-being (see Example A in Figure 5.1), which has a general effect on relationship quality. We might expect, if this interpretation is valid, to find that these children also had difficulties in other social relationships such as with their grandparents and fathers.

Other results in that Cambridge study indicated more specific or focused connections between the mother-child and sibling relationships. For instance, in families with firstborn girls in which relations between mother and first child had been particularly close, an especially hostile relationship developed between the siblings during the next year. In contrast, in families with considerable confrontation between child and mother before the sibling birth, the two siblings were particularly friendly toward each other 1 year later. A similar pattern of findings concerning father-firstborn and later sibling relationships was also suggested from interview findings. Two interpretations of the connections between relationships are suggested by this pattern of findings (they are not incompatible). We could view the hostile behavior of those firstborn girls who had enjoyed a close relationship with their mothers as a response to being supplanted: a hostile emotional response, but one more specific in focus than the disturbance suggested in the first instance (see Example B in Figure 5.1). But we could also focus on the high level of friendly warm behavior that is directed to the baby sibling by those children who had more detached or more conflicted relationships with their parents. Here the connection could be interpreted in terms of a general emotional kind (see Example B in Figure 5.1): We could conclude that a need for affection and attention can sometimes be met within the sibling relationship, especially for those children whose relationship with their mothers was either distant or confrontational.

Other findings from the research suggested more specific processes linking the relationships. In families in which a particularly close, warm relationship developed between mother and secondborn, a very hostile confrontational relationship was likely to develop between the firstborn and the sibling. The evidence for the vigilance with which both firstborn and laterborn children monitor the interaction between their parents and siblings, the promptness with which they react to it, and their explicit comments on mother-sibling interaction all indicate that some children witness the warm play between their mothers and siblings with considerable pain; this pain is linked to the development of a hostile relationship with the sibling. In the third process (Example C in Figure 5.1), focused hostility develops as a response to an affectionate relationship between others (see Howe & Ross, 1990, for very similar findings; the greater the maternal involvement in play and attention to either child, the less friendly the interaction between the siblings).

The close monitoring of parent-sibling relationships suggests a further process linking the three relationships discussed in Chapter 3. Children are sensitive to relative differences in the relationships that they and their siblings have with their mother. What matters, according to this view, is not simply the experience of witnessing the affection between your brother and your mother, but rather the perception that you are loved less (Example D in Figure 5.1). As we saw in Chapter 3, an accumulation of research with siblings of different ages repeatedly finds differential parental treatment to be linked to the quality of the sibling relationship. Differential affection may well be of special developmental significance here.

The final level of process that links the relationships suggested by our research is more cognitive and was brought to our attention initially by the striking differences between mother-child pairs in their discussion of family relationships and by differences between mothers in their "management" of the relationship. Differences between families in the extent to which mother and firstborn engaged in conversations about the baby sibling as a person with needs, desires, and feelings were linked to later differences in not only the first child's behavior to the baby, but also the baby's friendly behavior to the older child over time. The research suggests that even with very young children, communication about and interpretation of others' behavior and the articulation of that interpretation play an important part in influencing the developing relationship between family members (Example E in Figure 5.1). Notably similar results were reported in a Canadian study (Howe & Ross, 1990).

LESSONS FROM RESEARCH: MOTHER, SIBLING, AND CHILD

The lesson from this evidence from the mother-sibling-child trio early in the siblings' lives is that we should not assume that the mechanisms that link relationships are simple or few. Which we choose to emphasize will depend on our theoretical perspective and on the kinds of dimensions and measures that we have chosen in describing relationships. For instance, the possibility that processes of a cognitive-attributional nature may be important only became evident because we chose to include such measures of talk in our description of the relationships. Those researchers working within an attachment framework have posed the question about links between these relationships in terms of the security of the parent-child relationship and of the processes in which a model of close relationships is formed with the mother and then reenacted with others. The hypothesis is that children with secure mother-child relationships are most likely to form friendly nonantagonistic relationships with their siblings. Some results fit this hypothesis (Teti & Ablard, 1989; see also Bosso, 1985) and are consistent with the notion that children who are insecure "will re-enact aspects of the non-nurturant caregiver role in their relationship with each other" (Teti & Ablard, 1989). However, many aspects of sibling interaction in the Teti and Ablard study did not show relations to attachment status. The mixed pattern of results reinforces the argument that child-parent and child-sibling relationships are both complex and multidimensional; furthermore, although some facets of each relationship will show links with aspects of the other, we should not look for overall, simple equivalences.

And we cannot assume that attachment status played a causal role in the associations found, because other factors such as the children's temperament also could be implicated. Note also that 36% of the siblings in Teti's study differed in their attachment status, a proportion similar to that reported by Ward, Vaughn, and Robb (1988). Given the prediction from attachment theory that a mother's behavior to her children will be influenced by her perception of her own childhood experiences, this difference in siblings' attachment status is of some interest.

This first lesson—that we should not expect simple global links between parent-child and sibling-child relationships—is emphasized in findings from the research of Hinde and his colleagues on 4-year-olds observed with their mothers and siblings (Hinde, Tamplin, & Barrett, in press, a). They contrast two generalizations from folk psychology: First, if aspects of personality were cross-situationally consistent, then one might expect that a child who had a warm relationship with her or his mother would be likely to have a warm relationship with a sibling; second, a child who lacked a warm relationship with her or his mother might compensate by having one with a sibling. The relations between child-mother and child-sibling interactions in their studies do not fit either prediction and are considerably more complex. Hinde et al. conclude:

> Overall, these data indicate that the relations between child characteristics, child-mother interaction, and child-sibling interaction cannot satisfactorily be portrayed by generalizations of the type "4-year-olds who have good/bad relationships with their mothers have good/bad relationships with their siblings." It is essential, instead, to recognize that each relationship is multifaceted.

We note three other general points about the connections between relationships. The first concerns the direction of effects. In several of the sets of data on the mother-sibling triad from our research, inferences about such a direction cannot be made. For instance, in Example A of Figure 5.1, even if the perturbation in the mother-child relationship initially led to emotionally disturbed behavior in the firstborn, such behavior in turn probably increased difficulties in the mother-firstborn relationship. In Examples C and D, the mothers may have increased their affectionate interaction with the secondborn whose older siblings were continually hostile; the mothers thus may have tried to compensate or comfort the secondborn suffering at the hands of the older sibling. And in Example E, mothers whose children are getting along well probably discuss the feelings of the sibling more freely than do mothers who know that their children do not like one another. This point— that the quality of the sibling relationship can affect the parent-child relationship—is clearly borne out in other data from our sibling studies, such as the finding that mothers' reactions to sibling quarrels differed according to how their children had behaved toward one another 6 months earlier (Kendrick & Dunn, 1983).

A second point concerns individual differences between children. The relative importance of the different processes outlined in the figure may differ for different children. Consider, for instance, Example A: The temperament of the firstborn children was key in accounting for the nature and extent of emotional disturbance at the sibling birth. Processes B and C depended on the particular qualities of the relationships between mother and first or second child. And for the cognitive-attributional processes summarized in Example E, individual differences in the children's and mothers' personalities and attitudes again were key. Which processes are likely to be developmentally important will depend on individual differences in the children and in their relationships with their mothers.

The third point raised by these different relationship-linking processes concerns the developmental stage of the child. How does the child's developmental stage affect the relative importance of these different processes? For very young children, who are vulnerable to emotional disturbance, the processes involved in Example A are more likely to occur in relationships than they are with older children. The processes involved in Example E, however, are likely to become more important as children grow into middle childhood and adolescence. Research on siblings in middle childhood suggests moreover that the nature of their relationship may be less closely tied to issues of differential treatment by parents than in early childhood and that issues involving friendship and peer relations become more important, a point we return to in the next chapter.

Connections Between Family Relationships and Friendships

How are children's family relationships linked to the first close relationships they form with other children outside the family—their friends—in the preschool and early childhood years? We look first at parents and children.

Parent-Child and Child-Friend Relationships

The question of whether and how children's relationships with their parents and their friends are linked is of particular interest. On theoretical grounds we might well expect to find clear links between the quality of children's relationships with their parents and with their friends. Attachment theory, for example, predicts that close relationships outside the family will be influenced by earlier attachment quality, and social learning theory would also predict positive associations between family and friend relationships. Surprisingly, most research until now has focused on possible links between parent-child relationships and peer status or interaction with unfamiliar peers rather than on friendship. Because our interest here is in close relationships rather than peer popularity, the key points raised by this "peer group" research will be only briefly summarized. (For useful reviews of research on peer relations and parent-child relationships, see Asher & Coie, 1989; Parke & Ladd, 1992; see also Dunn & McGuire, 1992, and Parker & Asher, 1987.)

One general assumption holds that the foundations for children's relations with both friends and peers are laid in the emotional security and social skills that they develop in their family relationships—especially those with their mothers. The empirical grounds for this idea come from three types of study, each of which reveals some association between family and peer relations. Researchers have studied (1) the peer relations of institution-reared children who have experienced disrupted parenting or a lack of attachment relationships in childhood (Hodges & Tizard, 1989); (2) parental behavior and attitudes and their links to peer relations (mainly with cross-sectional studies of peer status); and (3) early attachment status and later behavior with peers (studies within an attachment framework).

The following general points from this large body of research are relevant to our theme here. First, correlations are frequently reported between some aspects of social behavior with peers and attachment quality; indeed, the evidence for associations between secure attachment and competence in peer interaction at the preschool stage is quite impressive (e.g., Cohn, Patterson, & Christopoulos, in press; Fagot & Kavanagh, 1990; Pierrehumbert, Ianotti, Cummings, & Zahn-Waxler, 1989; Sroufe, Egeland, & Kreutzer, 1990). The limitations of the data lie in the limited range of measures of relationships used, the narrowness of the contexts in which the children are studied, and the paucity of research on fathers with their children. The few studies of fathers and children suggest the possibility of important differences in the links between father-child and mother-child relationships and behavior with peers and that these links may differ between boys and girls (e.g., MacDonald & Parke, 1984; Youngblade, Park, & Belsky, submitted). Most important, causal links between attachment status and later peer behavior are not established.

Second, a wide variety of aspects of parent-child relations are thought to influence indirectly children's behavior with peers, such as parental emotional expressiveness (Cassidy, Parke, Butkovsky, & Braungart, 1992), attitudes (Roopnarine & Honig, 1985), discipline techniques (Baumrind, 1971; Dishion, Patterson, Stoolmiller, & Skinner, 1990), mental health (Zahn-Waxler, Denham, Ianotti, & Cummings, 1991), and support networks and life events that affect parents (Dishion, 1990; Masten, Garmezy, Tellegen, Pellegrini, Larkin, & Larsen, 1988; Patterson, Vaden, & Kupersmidt, in press). Parents' direct management of peer relations is also now a topic of interest (for a review, see Parke & Ladd, 1992), as is the impact of nonparental care in the early years (for reviews, see Hayes, Palmer, & Zaslow, 1990; McCartney, 1990). The intriguing findings of Hodges and Tizard (1989), who followed up children who had been in institutions in infancy, for instance, suggest the existence of long-term associations between early attachment experiences and problems with peers as 16-year-olds.

The findings of those few friendship studies (as opposed to studies of peer interaction or popularity) so far completed are intriguing, and they complement the points made by the parent-sibling research in a provocative way.

First, a study of 4-year-old best friend dyads showed that security of mother-child attachment (assessed when the friendship quality was being studied) was linked to "a relatively specific set of friendship correlates" (Park & Waters, 1989). Pairs of friends in which both children were securely attached to their mothers were more harmonious, more responsive, and less controlling than secure-insecure dyads. These friends did not engage in less conflict, but they were likely to negotiate disputes peacefully and distribute toys more equally.

However, research that examined 5-year-olds' friendships and earlier attachment relationships with both mothers and fathers raised several important questions about the links between the relationships. Youngblade, Park, and Belsky (submitted) report that "no significant relations were found between mother-child attachment and friendship regardless of whether attachment was measured with the Strange Situation or Attachment Q-set." Mother-child attachment at one year predicted subsequent relationships "only after contemporaneous experience is accounted for." Indeed, several findings in this study suggested that compensatory processes might be at work, raising the possibility that children compensate in their friendships for parent-child relationships that are not satisfying emotionally. This does suggest a link between parent-child and child-friend relationships, but not one in which there is a simple positive carry-over from one relationship to the next. The findings on father-child relationships make the picture even more complicated. First, they indicated the existence of more connections between the quality of the friendship and the father-child relationship than that of the mother-child relationship. However, very different patterns of association were seen, depending on how the attachment was measured—and, again, evidence showed compensatory patterns. Youngblade and her colleagues conclude that their findings underscore "the need to go beyond simply 'all-good-things-go-together' hypotheses" (Youngblade & Belsky, 1992), which is a recommendation to be strongly endorsed.

As we saw in Chapter 4, the children of our current study in Pennsylvania who had been observed with their mothers and siblings as preschoolers were studied as 47-month-olds and as 5-year-olds with a close friend. We examined the children's conflicts, their pretend play, and the connectedness and emotional expression of their communication and then compared differences in these relationship features with the quality of their relationships with mothers and siblings (e.g., Slomkowski & Dunn, 1992; Slomkowski & Dunn, submitted, a).

The results brought some surprises. For instance, we found no evidence for associations between the emotional quality of the children's relationships with their friends (either the expression of positive or negative emotion), the connectedness of their interactions, or the dimension of shared fantasy in their relationships, and the individual differences in their interactions with their mothers in terms of conflict or the expression of positive emotion. One important exception to this evidence for lack of connections across relationships was that children who grew up in families with frequent expressions of anger or distress tended not to reason at all in conflict with their friends; instead, they simply protested without argument or justification. However, children's strategies in handling conflict with their friends were not closely related to their interaction with their mothers in conflict. Those children who took account of their friend's position, who negotiated and made concessions or compromises particularly frequently, were not more likely than the rest of the sample to do so with their mothers. But some connections were evident with the dimension of mother-child involvement and the qualities of the children's interaction with their friends. Those children who had enjoyed a high degree of involvement with their mothers were more likely to use compromise and negotiation in their arguments with their friends. They were also the children whose connected communication with their friends was extensive, and they also enjoyed a high degree of shared fantasy play in their relationships.

The complexity of the patterns of association across parent-child and child-friend relationships does not decrease when we look at studies of older children. For example, Stocker and Mantz-Simmons (in press) found evidence for associations across the relationships in a study of 7-year-olds when the children were reporting on both of their relationships. Children who reported high levels of maternal warmth also reported more companionship, more positive behavior, and less conflict in their friendships than did other children. However, evidence for connections was less clear when parental reports or observations—as opposed to child self-report—were the source of information, but those significant correlations that were found (only 3 out of 30 performed) were in this same direction. And, interestingly, the pattern of links was different for mothers and fathers. Children whose relationships with their fathers were characterized by high controlling or uninvolved fathers were less likely to cooperate well with their friends than children who had highly involved or less controlling fathers. No such pattern was found for the mother-child relationship. Again, we are reminded that there may be closer links between father-child relations than mother-child relations and those with other children outside the family. Nonlinear relations between parent-child and child-friend relationships may not have been exposed by these analyses.

As for links between early attachment and friendships in middle childhood, Lewis and Feiring (1989) report only very limited support for connections between attachment quality in infancy and the number of close friends reported by 9-year-old children. This scattering of studies surely supports the argument made by Youngblade and her colleagues that, in looking for connections between parent-child and friend relationships, we need to go beyond simply hypothesizing that all good things go together.

A similar point is powerfully made by the results of a study by Hinde and his colleagues of 4-year-olds with their mothers, siblings, teachers, and peers (Hinde, Tamplin, & Barrett, in press, b). Children from different families who resembled one another in their parent-child relationships did not resemble one another in their other relationships outside the family. Hinde and his colleagues emphasize two key reasons why we should not expect close links across these relationships. First, the nature of the relationship depends on two participants who will differ in the different relationships; second, different aspects of A's personality may be relevant to A's relationship with B and with C. Hinde indeed found that different aspects of children's temperament were important in connection with the various relationships studied—as we did in our Pennsylvania study—and drew the following general conclusions:

> The nature of a relationship is affected by both participants, so an individual may well have different relationships with different partners. And beyond that, an aspect of personality relevant to one type of relationship may not be relevant to another type, so that individuals who had similar relationships of one type to which the trait in question was irrelevant, may have diverse relationships with a type of partner with whom it mattered. We suggest that inter-relationship coherence could more readily be identified if the differential effects of individual characteristics in different relationships could be brought into the equation. Thus this evidence implies that inter-relationship coherence is not necessarily present, but does not mean that we should cease to search for it. (Hinde et al., in press, b)

One final point concerning the issue of whether differences in parent-child relationships cause differences in children's friendships deserves emphasis. We need to differentiate between variations within a normal distribution and children at the extremes. The studies of institution-reared children and of monkeys reared in isolation suggest that individuals who have lacked the experience of continuous attachment relationships in their early years are likely to have problems in their relationships with peers later in life. Given that the monkeys in the isolation studies and the children studied by Hodges and Tizard had both experienced radical changes in their environments following early childhood, the evidence for links over time does suggest some sort of causal connection. But this does not necessarily imply a similar kind of connection within the normal range.

Sibling and Friend Relationships

The idea that the quality of the relationships that children form with peers and friends will be linked to the quality of their sibling relationships is one that would be supported not only by attachment theory, but also by both social learning theory and those who argue that an individual's personality characteristics will elicit similar responses from different people (Caspi & Elder, 1988). Although the mechanisms thought to underlie the links between the relationships differ in the different theoretical approaches, each does suggest positive associations between sibling and peer relationships. A social learning framework, for instance, suggests that children learn behavioral responses in their family that are generalized to their interactions with peers and friends (Parke, MacDonald, Beitel, & Bhavnagri, 1988; Putallaz, 1987), and what is learned with a sibling might be plausibly generalized to interaction with another familiar child outside the family.

However, in contrast to these suggestions that connections between sibling relationships and friendships might be expected, there are several lines of argument against the idea that individual differences in the relationships should be linked. For example, clear differences are seen in the nature of the relationships in question. Although both are close, dyadic relationships—*intimate* in the sense that children know both their siblings and their friends quite well—friendships involve a mutual commitment of affection, support, and trust, and obviously not all siblings feel this way about one another. From research that compares the behavior of children with friends and with siblings, we know that children in disputes are more likely to take account of their friends' views than they are when in conflict with their siblings (Slomkowski & Dunn, 1992), that they are more likely to reason and negotiate with friends than with siblings (Raffaelli, 1991), and that they judge moral transgressions quite differently according to whether a friend or sibling is involved (Slomkowski & Dunn, submitted, a). With friends, moreover, there is no rivalry for parental love and attention and no history of competitive comparison as is often the case with siblings. Perhaps, too, when children within a friendship pair come from different families, their previous experience in relationships differs, and the unique combination of these characteristics in a particular friendship decreases the likelihood that links between sibling and friendship relationships will be found.

How far do the results of the (relatively few) studies of sibling and friend relationships support either of these two points of view?

Consider first the evidence from the 4- to 6-year-old children in our Pennsylvania study. We compared a range of different features of their relationships with both sibling and friend: In their conflicts, for instance, we looked at the frequency of disputes, the strategies the children used, the emotions they expressed, the extent to which they reasoned and took the other child's point of view into account, and the outcome of the conflict. We also looked at their affectionate behavior, their engagement in joint pretend, and more generally their connected communication with these different partners.

What evidence did we find for connections between individual differences in the interactions with sibling and with friend? In general, we saw more correspondence in the children's argument style between their sibling and friend relationships than between their conflict styles with mothers and friends. Specifically, children who considered their siblings' interests in disputes when they were 33 months old tended to take their friends' point of view into account in conflicts with them 14 months later. (Note, however,

CHILD-SIBLING
RELATIONSHIP

CHILD-FRIEND
RELATIONSHIP

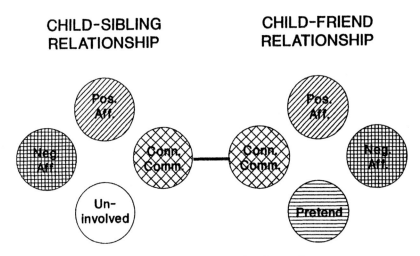

Figure 6.1. Child-Sibling and Child-Friend Relationships.

that children who rarely made compromises or negotiated and who instead argued in their own self-interest commonly behaved notably differently with their friends and considered the others' wishes or goals.) And children who frequently did not reason at all in disputes with their friends and simply yelled their protests tended to behave the same way with their siblings.

An association also was found between differences in the dimension of connected communication in sibling and friend relationships. Children who engaged in long, connected conversations with their siblings were likely to do so with their friends. Figure 6.1 illustrates the links—and lack of connections—among the four dimensions derived from factor analysis for the child-sibling and child-friend relationships, respectively.

The differences between the two relationships were in other respects clear. As Figure 6.1 indicates, no association was found between the emotional quality of the two relationships; the correlates of the various dimensions also were different. Different aspects of temperament, for example, were linked to conflict style and connectedness with friend and with sibling (as in the study by Hinde and colleagues referred to above). Studying the children in the context of first one relationship and then the other brought home to us how different the two relationships frequently were. As we saw earlier, children's views on the permissibility of moral transgressions in the two relationships were, for example, notably different (Slomkowski & Dunn, submitted, b). Other studies of children in this age range also report no associations between the two relationships (Abramovitch, Corter, Pepler, & Stanhope, 1986).

We found one exception to this picture. In families with frequent expressions of anger or distress by family members—whether children, siblings, or mothers—we found more links across the children's relationships. In these families, the children were especially likely not to reason or negotiate in conflict with both sibling and friend; they simply protested without providing any reason, justification, or excuse for their position. The results raise the possibility that different patterns of links across relationships may exist for children who are growing up in families that are toward the extremes of emotional behavior or under particular stress—at least in terms of their conflict interactions (see Radke-Yarrow, Richters, & Wilson, 1988).

Studies of slightly older children have found links between certain aspects of the sibling and friend relationships but not others. For instance, one study of 7- and 8-year-olds reports that children who were relatively controlling with their siblings also were controlling and less positive about their friends when interviewed about their relationship than were other children. Children who were particularly cooperative with their siblings were also especially cooperative and affectionate with their friends (the observations being made at the same time here) (Stocker & Mantz-Simmons, in press). However, the pattern of findings was not a simple one: For instance, children who were observed to be particularly cooperative with their siblings reported lower levels of companionship with friends. The investigators' interpretation of these findings was that children who are close to their siblings may choose to spend less time and be involved in fewer activities with their friends than other children and thus report low levels of the "companionship" aspects of the relationship. The researchers also point out that parents of these children may be less motivated to arrange for their children to play with friends when compared with siblings' parents who have hostile and quarrelsome relationships.

Evidence for "compensatory" patterns, rather than consistency across the two relationships, was found in two other studies. The firstborn children in the Colorado Sibling Study were studied with their siblings and friends in middle childhood, and the results showed that children who were particularly competitive and controlling with their younger siblings were more positive with their friends than with other children (Stocker & Dunn, 1990). Why should the results of this study differ from those of the Stocker and Mantz-Simmons research in the pattern of links between controlling behavior shown to a sibling and positive affection for a friend? One possibility is that the birth order of the children is important. The significance of controlling behavior to a sibling may be very different for firstborn and laterborn children. Controlling behavior with a younger sibling is an expected pattern for a firstborn—and also not inconsistent with being very positive to a friend. In the Colorado Sibling Study analyses, the children were indeed firstborn. In contrast, many of the children in the study by Stocker and Mantz-Simmons were secondborn, and for a secondborn child to be controlling to an older sibling may suggest a controlling or combative personality that is also less likely to be cooperative and positive with a friend.

Further evidence that negative sibling relationships were associated with positive friendships was reported by Mendelson and his colleagues (Mendelson & Aboud, 1991). Both observations and self-report measures of kindergartners' interactions with siblings and friends showed this pattern of results for same-sex siblings with same-sex friends, but not for opposite-sex siblings. A variety of interpretations for these results was offered. For instance, a child who feels positively about a same-sex sibling may be less motivated to develop same-sex friendships, although a child who has the same feelings for an other-sex sibling may still seek out same-sex friendships, which are the norm for children of this age (Maccoby, 1990). A second interpretation is that positive feelings for an older or younger sibling lead to skills or expectations that are not very suitable for interacting with same-aged friends; for instance, children who are used to a close relationship with an older sibling may expect their friends to take the initiative.

LESSONS FROM RESEARCH ON SIBLINGS AND FRIENDS

In summary, four general lessons stand out from these studies of friends and siblings in early and middle childhood. First, we see some consistencies in children's behavior in their relationships with their friends and siblings, although by no means is it a simple carry-over from one relationship to the other; indeed, considerable evidence is seen for inconsistency across the relationships. We could interpret the lack of consistency in a variety of ways: by invoking either compensatory mechanisms or the suggestion that through the experience of competitive or controlling interaction with their siblings children develop capacities in social understanding that equip them to form particularly close relationships with their friends. For example, the Pennsylvania study provided evidence that the experience of frequent argument with a sibling is correlated with later success on sociocognitive tasks (Slomkowski & Dunn, 1992); we cannot, however, make causal inferences from these correlational data.

Second, the developmental stage of the children should be taken into account in looking for connections across the relationships. In a study of 3-year-old firstborn children, for instance, Kramer (1990) found that the children with closer, more "connected" friendships were more positive toward their infant siblings in the early months following the siblings' birth. We could see this as evidence for the supportive role that friendships can play for young children: The relatively friendly behavior of the 3-year-olds with good friendships toward the new siblings might reflect a better adjustment to the upheaval surrounding their arrival. However, extrapolating from the behavior of a 3-year-old to a baby sibling to the interaction of 10- to 12-year-old siblings would be hazardous. In the case of a 3-year-old and a new baby sibling, the interaction is between two individuals who have drastically different communicative competencies and understanding and who play notably different parts in the interaction. What makes for harmonious interaction between a 3-year-old and a 3-month-old is likely to be very different from the factors implicated in harmonious relations between 10- and 12-year-olds. In addition, the birth order of the siblings needs to be considered in interpreting some dimensions of the relationship, such as controlling, dominating behavior; gender also may be important to consider, at least beyond the preschool years.

Third, very few associations are found between children's sibling relationships and their popularity with peers, either at the preschool stage (Berndt & Bulleit, 1985) or as 5- to 10-year-olds (Stocker & Dunn, 1990). Some correlations are reported for aggression with siblings and with peers (Vandell, Minnett, Johnson, & Santrock, 1990), and gender differences may exist in the patterns of association between siblings' relationships and peer popularity by the time children reach adolescence (East, 1989).

Fourth, children's temperamental characteristics may be responsible for some of the links reported between the relationships (Stevenson-Hinde, Hinde, & Simpson, 1986; Stocker & Dunn, 1990), although the personalities of both children in a friendship dyad and both children in the sibling pair probably need to be taken into account in looking for connections across the relationships. To date, no studies have included the information on all three interactants.

Processes Linking the Relationships

What are the implications of these empirical findings on associations—or lack of associations—between children's different relationships for the various current ideas on the processes or mechanisms linking relationships? We will look at some of the candidates that have been suggested to play a role in the mechanisms that link relationships.

INTERNAL WORKING MODELS

To explain how children developed attachments that later influenced their relationships, Bowlby (1969) proposed the idea that children develop—from infancy onward—increasingly complex internal representations of their relationships with significant others (see also Craik, 1943). From their initial relationship with their primary caregivers, Bowlby suggested, children developed cognitive models of self, other, and the relationship between them; these internal working models then were seen as playing a key role in influencing the quality of later relationships. Bowlby saw these internal working models as "none other than the 'internal worlds' of traditional psychoanalytic theory seen in a new perspective" (Bowlby, 1982, p. 82).

The idea has been taken up with great enthusiasm. Part of the resulting excitement and widespread interest stems from the proposal's heuristic value: It suggests a potential linking of cognitive psychologists' ideas on mental models with basic psychoanalytic views on the significance of mother-child relationships, as well as with the growing interest in children's social understanding. The notion of a working model includes the idea of possible changes over time, and part of the attraction of this proposed mechanism lies in its bringing together of cognitive and affective aspects of development.

How useful is such a model in explaining the patterns of findings on children's early relationships? Paradoxically, one limitation with the idea of the internal working model is that it is so vaguely conceived that it can be used to explain almost everything. What exactly is an internal working model? The answers range widely. It has been described as "a mental representation of an aspect of the world, others, self, or relationships to others that is of special relevance to the individual" (Main, Kaplan, & Cassidy, 1985, p. 68); it is variously seen as filtering input from the outside world and as directing activity and responses; as a set of conscious or unconscious rules for organizing information about relationships; as self-perpetuating and resistant to change and yet as modifiable. It has been described as a hierarchical network of representations of increasing specificity, and different internal working models have been seen as themselves hierarchically organized, with the mother-child relationship heading the tier and being more potent in influencing later relationships than that of the father-child relationship. And an individual may, according to some writers, have more than one internal working model of the same relationship. Crittenden and her colleagues (Crittenden, Partridge, & Claussen, 1992), for instance, write of three internal models for each relationship and a "metamodel" over them all. According to some, discrepancies between the models sometimes lead to psychopathology.

As Hinde (1988) notes, "It is difficult to avoid the conclusion that properties are added to the working model as new phenomena require explanation, and that at least some of the new properties are isomorphic with the phenomena they purport to explain" (p. 379). As a proposed mechanism, it does not lead to any directly testable, falsifiable hypotheses about the pattern of findings found in studies of relationships. It does not help us to get closer to understanding which aspects of relationships with parents might be linked to which dimensions of children's other relationships. Indeed, its very generality moves us in the wrong direction: away from focusing on the different kinds of processes involved in the links between relationships—such as the processes suggested in the discussion of the mother-sibling-child triad (Chapter 5)—and away from the rigors of becoming more precise about the nature of connections.

Furthermore, although some kind of mental representation of children's various relationships must be developing over the first, second, and third year, we are very far from understanding what properties such cognitive representations are likely to possess at various ages. It certainly seems hard to reconcile what we know of 12-month-olds' cognitive abilities with what must be involved in representing both sides of a relationship, as Sroufe and Fleeson (1986) suggest the internal working model entails. At a theoretical level, Bretherton's (1990) conceptualization of internal working models as "more or less well organized webs of hierarchically structured information (embedded in and connected to other schema hierarchies stored in long-term memory)" (p. 248) suggests a more flexible, differentiated way of thinking about what is represented, and it also makes the reworking of internal models of relationships more understandable than do some accounts. However, the vagueness and generality of the metaphors commonly used to describe internal working models of relationships stand in especially sharp contrast to the precision of description and thought that is the common currency of those who are attempting to understand what children understand about mental states (e.g., Astington, Harris, & Olson, 1989; Frye & Moore, 1991; Whiten, 1991).

The idea of internal working models, then, does not appear to give us any increased precision in understanding either the patterns of association found between sibling and friend relationships or why closer connections should be found between father-child and friend relationships than between mother-child relationships and friendships.

SOCIAL UNDERSTANDING AS A MEDIATOR

One frequently offered interpretation to explain connections between family relationships and children's relations with their peer group is that children who have trouble with their peers have problems in social-information processing and that these socio-cognitive "deficits" stem from their experiences with their parents. The immediate causes of the difficulties of children who are disliked, neglected, or aggressive toward their peers or who have trouble joining groups of peers are thought to reflect deficits in social-processing skills (Rubin, Bream, & Rose-Krasnor, in press). Several mechanisms have been suggested to be involved in the connections between such deficits and parent-child relationships: for example, parental disciplinary styles affect children's problem-solving skills and reasoning, which then affects their interactions with peers (Pettit, Harrist, Bates, & Dodge, in press); parental emotional expressiveness influences children's emotional understanding, and this in turn influences their peer relations (Cassidy et al., 1992); the quality of parental sensitivity and responsiveness affects children's attachment relationships, and these in turn influence their social competence; and a general stress model provides the link (Patterson et al., in press).

These ideas were all formulated in relation to children's peer acceptance and popularity rather than their friendships. How useful are they for understanding the connections between family relationships and friendships? In particular, how do they fit with the recent studies of social understanding in young children?

First, the recent work on social understanding highlights the considerable powers of even very young children. From early in the preschool years, most children recognize and respond to the feelings of others and behave practically to improve or worsen other people's emotional state. They understand the connections between others' beliefs and desires, and their behavior. They have some grasp of what is appropriate moral behavior for different relationships. Such sophistication means that even young children can be supportive, concerned, intimate, and humorous with others—or they can be manipulative, devious, and teasing and deliberately upset others. Most important, the same child could put these capabilities to use in very different ways in different relationships. (The evidence for subtlety in social interactions does not mean that these young children have power to reflect on or "metacognize" in any elaborate way about their relationships or that they have an accessible "model" of relationships.) The evidence shows clearly that marked individual differences can be found among children in their powers of social understanding (Dunn, Brown, & Beardsall, 1991). Do these differences in understanding others' emotions and behavior help to explain connections between relationships?

Two points stand out from the currently available evidence on family relationships and friendships. First, evidence exists for connections between individual differences in social understanding as assessed formally—as an individual characteristic—and children's behavior in their close relationships. For instance, in the Pennsylvania Sibling Study, we found significant correlations between performance on social cognition tasks and some aspects of children's interactions with mothers, siblings, and friends. Success on tests of understanding "other minds," for example, was associated with engagement in shared pretend and with the use of compromise and negotiation in conflict with siblings 7 months earlier (Slomkowski & Dunn, 1992; Youngblade & Dunn, submitted) and with connectedness in interaction with a close friend 7 months later (Slomkowski & Dunn, submitted, a).

However, our second point is that evidence also exists that children use their powers of social understanding very differently in different relationships, according to the emotional quality of those different relationships (as we saw in Chapter 5). We come back to the point that the quality of relationships depends on both partners and is unlikely to be attributable simply to the sociocognitive skills of one partner. Indeed, the nature of social understanding that children show within a relationship can be considered an "emergent property" of that relationship, one that depends on both partners.

Much more work remains to be done before we can reach clear conclusions about the ways in which children's social understanding is linked to different aspects of their relationships. For instance, for children at the extremes of sociocognitive skills or those in stressful family relationships, the links between social cognitive abilities and relationships may be different (probably stronger) than the connections within the rest of the population. We should also remember that the issue of direction of effects remains a puzzle. For instance, children probably develop sociocognitive skills in the context of their relationships with other children outside the family; these skills then influence the quality of their family relationships.

FAMILY SOCIALIZATION MODELS AND GENETIC MEDIATION

Other explanations of connections between parent-child and peer relationships include the proposal that it is differences in parental modeling or teaching that influence children's peer relations or that parents indirectly influence these relations through setting up situations in which children can develop relationships with other children. Putallaz and Heflin (1990) cite four different mechanisms of direct influence of parents: modeling, operant conditioning, classical conditioning, and coaching. All appear plausible; we have no evidence for their relative importance in explaining connections between children's experiences in real-life families and friendships. What we do have evidence for now is the significance of genetic "confounds" in such associations.

Any correlation between measures of family relationships or experiences and children's relationships with peers or friends could, of course, result from a third common causal factor. And genetics may indeed play such a role. It appears quite plausible that for genetic reasons a child could be sociable with both parents and siblings and friends. And genetics could also contribute to an association between a warm sociable parent and a child who is warm and sociable with his or her friends. As Rowe (1989) notes, phenotypes can be matched simply because genotypes are incidentally matched.

Adoption studies allow us to test such a possibility by comparing the associations found in families in which parents and children are genetically related with the associations found in families in which adopted children do not share segregating genes with their parents. Twin studies in which the environments of identical and fraternal twins are compared also test these possibilities. Such comparisons have revealed genetic influences on a wide range of measures of aspects of family environments, including, as we saw in Chapter 2, measures of parental behavior toward their children and ratings by parents and children of their family environment. These comparisons also have shown genetic influences on ratings of peer groups, life events, and social support (Plomin & Neiderhiser, 1992). On average, heritability estimates for such environmental measures are approximately .30, which suggests that genetics can account for more than one quarter of the variance of these measures. And the possibility that links between measures of family environment and children's outcome were mediated through genetics has now been tested directly.

For example, a recent report examined associations between measures of the home environment and mental development in infants with a study of adoptive and nonadoptive children (Braungart, Plomin, & Fulker, in press). Path analysis was compatible with the view that genetic factors accounted for one half of the association between the environmental measure and the measure of mental development. In similar fashion, some theorists have argued that the links between family environment and sociometric status also may involve genetic mediation (Rowe, 1989). As yet, we do not know how far the complex associations between family relationships and friendships also involve genetic mediation, but clearly such possibilities must be investigated.

In summary, very different mechanisms have been postulated as mediating connections between family and friend relationships, and each explanation has its own compatible evidence. To assess their relative importance, we need research that allows us to examine the hypotheses for each of these processes concurrently; in this way we can judge their differing explanatory powers.

Relationships in Action

It is widely agreed that the quality of children's relationships in early childhood can be centrally important in their development. Yet these relationships have been studied chiefly within a relatively narrow paradigm. Our inspection of children's early relationships with their parents, siblings, and friends leads to the following points of argument.

CHILDREN'S RELATIONSHIPS ARE MULTIDIMENSIONAL

First, even in the preschool years, children's relationships with others are complex and involve a range of different dimensions, including connectedness, shared humor, balance of control, intimacy, and shared positive emotions. The recent work on young children's social understanding shows us how relevant these dimensions are, even for young children. Patterns of individual differences in relationships involve more than is indicated by a typology of attachment security, which assigns children to four groups. Relationships with mothers, fathers, siblings, and friends differ in structure and quality, and each involves several dimensions.

The lesson to be drawn from this first point is that we must broaden the framework within which we study relationships to appreciate both the nature of children's relationships and their developmental implications. The attachment framework has been useful in illuminating aspects of the parent-child relationships and their significance in later life, as well as in setting up hypotheses about what processes may be important. However, its typology is both limited and limiting.

CHILDREN'S RELATIONSHIPS CHANGE WITH DEVELOPMENT

Second, these relationships change in nature as children grow up. New dimensions of intimacy, self-disclosure, and shared intimacy become apparent over the early years, reflecting children's growing social understanding. These developments bring new sources and new patterns of individual differences in close relationships as children develop.

Here the lesson to be drawn is that our framework for describing relationships should be sensitive to developmental change, rather than focused solely on evidence for stability of dimensions over time or changes in response to external events or stresses.

BOTH PARTNERS IN THE RELATIONSHIP CONTRIBUTE TO ITS QUALITY

Third, both partners in a relationship contribute to its qualities, and no aspect of either partner's behavior in a relationship can be assumed to be independent of the shared history of their relationship together. Yet in the study of parent-child relationships, the interpretive weight has been put on the mother as the source of individual differences in the relationship. This emphasis reflects the origins of the study of parent-child relationships in psychoanalytic theory; it rarely reflects the results of rigorous empirical assessment of the contribution of individual differences in children to the relationship, consideration of the significance of continuing social circumstances on both partners, or even comparison of the significance of mothers' versus fathers' relationships with children in early childhood.

The lesson here is that we need a more critical consideration of the contribution of individual differences in children to differences in the quality of their relationships. Research using such approaches as the social relations model (Kenny & La Voie, 1984) would be especially fruitful, although as Hinde (personal communication) points out, this model, which assesses group variance, leads away from study of the individual.

THE CONNECTIONS BETWEEN RELATIONSHIPS ARE NOT SIMPLE OR GLOBAL

Fourth, we should not expect—and we are unlikely to find—simple, strong connections between different relationships of a global kind. The nature, structure, dynamics, demands, and rewards of children's relationships with parents, siblings, and friends are different in important respects, and the quality of each depends on both individuals involved in the particular relationship. The evidence suggests many different kinds of processes can be involved in patterns of links between relationships.

One (probably provocative) conclusion that I draw from the material discussed is that differences in mother-child relationships do not link in a simple global way to differences in children's other relationships. A second conclusion is that we need to move away from general claims about relations among relationships, and from attributing connections between relationships to vaguely conceived general mechanisms such as internal working models, toward specifying for *which* children at *which* stages of development, *which* dimensions of particular relationships are likely to show associations with other relationships. Specific hypotheses could be set up and tested. For example, attachment security with parents will be linked to differences in intimacy and trust in later peer relationships, but not to companionship, humor, or shared fantasy. And children who experience parent-child relationships characterized by much discussion of feelings, psychological causality, and self-disclosure are likely to be relatively sophisticated in their emotional understanding, although this understanding will be used in very different ways in their various later relationships and will not increase the likelihood, for example, of mutual affection in friendship. Different aspects of children's personalities are evident in different relationships, and such temperamental characteristics can lead to some similarities in the quality of different relationships (across different child-friend relationships, for instance) and to marked differences across other relationships (child-teacher, child-sibling, and child-friend, for instance).

SOCIAL UNDERSTANDING IS MORE THAN A WITHIN-CHILD CHARACTERISTIC

Recent evidence on the nature and development of children's social understanding has many implications for the study of relationships. First, such evidence has shown that children are sensitive to and influenced by the quality of interaction and relationships between others in the family—and quite possibly those outside the family. Second, it has shown that processes of self-evaluation and social comparison are evident in early childhood in the context of relationships; furthermore, dimensions of self-disclosure, criticism, and comparison are important in such early relationships. Third, children use their resources of social understanding differently in different social relationships, depending on the nature and emotional quality of those relationships.

One lesson from this evidence is that the significant developmental influences on children include not only the direct interaction of others with them, but also the quality and nature of relationships between others in their world and the relative affection, appreciation, and control they receive. If we are serious about trying to understand developmental influences, we should include in our investigations a focus on children's responses to these other relationships. For example, why and how are differences in the quality of marital relationships linked to differences in children's outcome? Our research on the question should be structured to examine both the links between marital and parent-child relationships—as well as the response of children to the relationship between their parents.

Not only do children observe and respond to the behavior directed toward them, but also they are family members, in a deep sense, from their first year.

Second, we should move away from the notion of social competence as solely an individual within-child trait that acts as a mediating link across relationships; instead we might see social understanding as it is expressed in interaction as closely bound— in practice—to the quality of particular aspects of particular relationships, as an emergent property of relationships, as well as a trait that the child carries from relationship to relationship.

Third, we should appreciate that the development of social understanding can be influenced by differences in the quality of not only parent-child but also sibling-child and friend-child relationships.

PREDICTIONS FROM RELATIONSHIP QUALITIES MUST BE MORE PRECISE

Consider the evidence for the multidimensional nature of children's relationships; the different structure of relationships with parents, siblings, and friends; and the marked individual differences in each. This has implications for the conclusions we attempt to draw concerning links between relationships and children's outcome. For instance, growing evidence (correlational, and therefore limited in what we can conclude about causality) exists for the particular role of experiences of cooperation with an older sibling in sociocognitive development (e.g., Dunn & Dale, 1984; Dunn, Brown, Slomkowski, Tesla, & Youngblade, 1991); similarly, experiences of shared talk about feelings with mothers are implicated in the understanding of emotions (Dunn, Brown, & Beardsall, 1991). The lesson is that we should move toward posing precise questions about the significance of particular dimensions of particular relationships for individual outcome, rather than making predictions from global characterizations of relationship quality, if we are to get purchase on the difficult developmental questions concerning outcome.

Strength of Conclusions

Are these conclusions wrong? The value and usefulness of these lessons can be tested, and each argument can be shown as unsupported *if and only if* we design our studies so that we can test a variety of different hypotheses about the significance of children's relationships. Consider two examples.

First, the argument that particular dimensions of relationships—rather than global affective characteristics—are significant for particular aspects of other relationships or outcome can be shown to be wrong if we test it with research that includes measures of both global and specific features of relationships. Does security of attachment better explain individual differences in social understanding than more specific dimensions of parent-child relationships such as discourse about the social world? Are some sibling relationships of particular importance in the development of social understanding but not in cognitive or language development? Quite possibly the evidence will show that some hypotheses are supported for children growing up in some circumstances (comfortable, stress-free, middle-class families) but not for children growing up in more stressful circumstances.

Second, we can test whether the evidence that how an individual child uses his or her social understanding within particular relationships differs according to other qualities of those relationships is more—or less—powerful than the evidence for the argument that social understanding acts instead as a "mediator" connecting parent-child, sibling, and peer relationships.

A broad framework, an appreciation of the richness and complexity of these relationships and the subtlety of children's social understanding, and a critical posing of alternative hypotheses will be needed if we are to gain a fuller understanding of children's relationships. Because they are the contexts within which all major childhood developments take place, these relationships surely deserve our careful attention and critical thought.

References

Abramovitch, R., Corter, C., Pepler, D. J., & Stanhope, L. (1986). Sibling and peer interaction: A final follow-up and a comparison. *Child Development, 57*, 217-229.

Achenbach, T. M., & Edelbrock, C. S. (1983). *Manual for the Child Behavior Checklist and Revised Child Behavior Profile*. Burlington: University of Vermont Press.

Adler, A. (1959). *Understanding human nature*. New York: Premier.

Ainsworth, M. D. S., Blehar, M. C., Waters, E., & Wall, S. (1978). *Patterns of attachment: A psychological study of the strange situation*. Hillsdale, NJ: Lawrence Erlbaum.

Ainsworth, M. D. S., & Bowlby, J. (1991). An ethological approach to personality development. *American Psychologist, 46*, 333-341.

Ainsworth, M. D. S., & Wittig, B. A. (1969). Attachment and exploratory behavior of one-year-olds in a strange situation. In B. M. Foss (Ed.), *Determinants of infant behaviour* (Vol. 4, pp. 111-136). London: Methuen.

Asher, S. R., & Coie, J. D. (1989). *Peer rejection in childhood*. New York: Cambridge University Press.

Astington, J. W., Harris, P. L., & Olson, D. R. (1989). *Developing theories of mind*. Cambridge, UK: Cambridge University Press.

Baskett, L. M., & Johnson, S. M. (1982). The young child's interactions with parents versus siblings: A behavioral analysis. *Child Development, 53*, 643-650.

Baumrind, D. (1971). Current patterns of parental authority. *Developmental Psychology Monographs, 4* (No. 1, Part 2).

Belsky, J. (1978). Three theoretical models of child abuse: A critical review. *International Journal of Child Abuse and Neglect, 2*, 37-49.

Belsky, J. (1984). The determinants of parenting: A process model. *Child Development, 55*, 83-96.

Belsky, J. (1990). Parental and nonparental care and children's socioemotional development. *Journal of Marriage and the Family, 52*, 885-903.

119

Belsky, J., & Cassidy, J. (in press). Attachment: Theory and evidence. In M. Rutter, D. Hay, & S. Baron-Cohen (Eds.), *Developmental principles and clinical issues in psychology and psychiatry*. Oxford, UK: Blackwell.

Belsky, J., Gilstrap, B., & Rovine, M. (1984). The Pennsylvania Infant and Family Development Project: I. Stability and change in mother-infant and father-infant interaction in a family setting at one, three, and nine months. *Child Development, 55,* 692-705.

Belsky, J., & Nezworski, T. (Eds.). (1988). *Clinical implications of attachment*. Hillsdale, NJ: Lawrence Erlbaum.

Belsky, J., & Rovine, M. (1988). Temperament and attachment security in the strange situation: An empirical rapprochement. *Child Development, 58,* 787-795.

Belsky, J., & Volling, B. L. (1987). Mothering, fathering, and marital interaction in the family triad during infancy: Exploring family systems processes. In P. Berman & F. Pedersen (Eds.), *Men's transition to parenthood* (pp. 37-63). Hillsdale, NJ: Lawrence Erlbaum.

Bernal-Dunn, J. F., & Richards, M. P. M. (1979). Observations on the developing relationship between mother and baby in the newborn period. In H. R. Schaffer (Ed.), *Studies in parent-infant interaction* (pp. 427-455). London: Academic Press.

Bernard, J. S. (1982). *The future of marriage*. New Haven, CT: Yale University Press.

Berndt, T. J. (1986). Sharing between friends: Contexts and consequences. In E. C. Mueller & C. R. Cooper (Eds.), *Process and outcome in peer relationships* (pp. 105-127). New York: Academic Press.

Berndt, T. J., & Bulleit, T. N. (1985). Effects of sibling relationships on preschoolers' behavior at home and at school. *Developmental Psychology, 21,* 761-767.

Berndt, T. J., Hawkins, J. A., & Hoyle, S. G. (1986). Changes in friendship during a school year: Effects on children's and adolescents' impressions of friendship and sharing with friends. *Child Development, 57,* 1284-1297.

Berndt, T. J., & Ladd, G. W. (1989). *Peer relationships in child development*. New York: John Wiley.

Berndt, T. J., & Perry, T. B. (1986). Children's perceptions of friendships as supportive relationships. *Developmental Psychology, 22,* 640-648.

Berndt, T. J., & Perry, T. B. (1990). Distinctive features and effects of early adolescent friendships. In R. Montemayor, G. R. Adams, & T. P. Gullotta (Eds.), *From childhood to adolescence: A translation period?* (pp. 269-287). Newbury Park, CA: Sage.

Berscheid, E. (1986). Emotional experience in close relationships: Some implications for child development. In W. W. Hartup & Z. Rubin (Eds.), *Relationships and development* (pp. 135-166). Hillsdale, NJ: Lawrence Erlbaum.

Blum, L. (1987). Particularity and responsiveness. In J. Kagan & S. Lamb (Eds.), *The emergence of morality in young children* (pp. 306-337). Chicago: University of Chicago Press.

Boer, F. (1990). *Sibling relationships in middle childhood*. Leiden, Germany: DSWO University of Leiden Press.

Boer, F., & Dunn, J. (Eds.). (1992). *Children's relationships with siblings: Developmental and clinical issues*. Hillsdale, NJ: Lawrence Erlbaum.

Bornstein, M. H. (1991). *Cultural approaches to parenting*. Hillsdale, NJ: Lawrence Erlbaum.

Bosso, R. (1985). Attachment quality and sibling relations: Responses of anxiously attached/avoidant and securely attached 18 to 32 month old firstborns towards their secondborn siblings. *Dissertation Abstracts International, 47*, 1293-B.

Bowlby, J. (1969). *Attachment and loss: Vol. 1. Attachment.* New York: Basic Books.

Bowlby, J. (1973). *Attachment and loss: Vol. 2. Separation: Anxiety and anger.* New York: Basic Books.

Bowlby, J. (1982). *Attachment and loss: Vol. 1. Attachment* (2nd ed.). London: Hogarth.

Bowlby, J. (1988). *A secure base.* New York: Basic Books.

Braungart, J. M., Plomin, R., Fulker, D. W., & De Fries, J. C. (in press). Genetic mediation of the home environment during infancy: A sibling adoption study of the HOME. *Developmental Psychology.*

Bretherton, I. (1990). Communication patterns, internal working models, and the intergenerational transmission of attachment relationships. *Infant Mental Health Journal, 11*, 237-252.

Bretherton, I., & Waters, E. (1985). Growing points in attachment theory and research. *Monographs of the Society for Research in Child Development, 50* (Serial No. 209).

Brody, G. H., Pillegrini, A. D., & Sigel, I. (1986). Marital quality and mother-child and father-child interaction with school-aged children. *Developmental Psychology, 22*, 291-296.

Brody, G. H., & Stoneman, Z. (1987). Sibling conflict: Contributions of the siblings themselves, the parent-sibling relationship, and the broader family system. *Journal of Children in Contemporary Society, 19*, 39-53.

Brody, G. H., Stoneman, Z., & Burke, M. (1987). Child temperaments, maternal differential behavior, and sibling relationships. *Developmental Psychology, 23*, 354-362.

Brown, G. W., & Harris, T. (1978). *Social origins of depression.* London: Tavistock.

Brown, J., & Dunn, J. (1991). "You can cry, Mom": The social and developmental implications of talk about internal states. *The British Journal of Developmental Psychology, 9*, 237-256.

Brown, J., & Dunn, J. (1992). Talk with your mother or your sibling? Developmental changes in early family conversations about feelings. *Child Development, 63*, 336-349.

Bruner, J. (1983). *Child's talk.* New York: Norton.

Bryant, P. (1985). Parents, children and cognitive development. In R. A. Hinde, A. N. Perret-Clermont, & J. Stevenson-Hinde (Eds.), *Social relationships and cognitive development* (pp. 239-251). Oxford, UK: Oxford University Press.

Buhrmester, D. (1992). The developmental courses of sibling and peer relationships. In F. Boer & J. Dunn (Eds.), *Children's sibling relationships: Developmental and clinical issues* (pp. 19-40). Hillsdale, NJ: Lawrence Erlbaum.

Buhrmester, D., & Furman, W. (1990). Perceptions of sibling relationships in childhood and adolescence. *Child Development, 61*, 1387-1398.

Bukowski, W. M., Hoza, B., & Newcomb, A. F. (1987). *Friendship, popularity and the "self" during adolescence.* Unpublished manuscript.

Burlingham, D., & Freud, A. (1944). *Infants without families.* London: Allen & Unwin.

Caspi, A., & Elder, G. H., Jr. (1988). Emergent family patterns: The intergenerational construction of problem behaviour and relationships. In R. A. Hinde & J. Stevenson-Hinde (Eds.), *Relationships within families: Mutual influences* (pp. 218-240). Oxford, UK: Clarendon.

Cassidy, J., & Asher, S. R. (1992). Loneliness and peer relations in young children. *Child Development, 63,* 350-365.

Cassidy, J., Parke, R. D., Butkowsky, L., & Braungart, J. (1992). Family-peer connections: The roles of emotional expressiveness within the family and children's understanding of emotions. *Child Development, 63,* 603-618.

Christensen, A., & Margolin, G. (1988). Conflict and alliance in distressed and non-distressed families. In R. A. Hinde & J. Stevenson-Hinde (Eds.), *Relationships within families: Mutual influences* (pp. 263-282). Oxford, UK: Clarendon.

Clarke-Stewart, K. A. (1989). Infant daycare: Malignant or maligned? *American Psychologist, 44,* 266-274.

Clarke-Stewart, K. A., & Hevey, C. M. (1981). Longitudinal relations in repeated observations of mother-child interactions from 1 to 2 and a half years. *Developmental Psychology, 17,* 127-145.

Clifford, E. (1959). Discipline in the home: A controlled observational study of parental practices. *Journal of Genetic Psychology, 95,* 45-82.

Cohn, D. A., Patterson, C. J., & Christopoulos, C. (in press). The family and children's peer relations. *Journal of Social and Personal Relationships.*

Cooper, C. R., Grotevant, H. D., & Condon, S. M. (1983). Individuality and connectedness in the family as a context for adolescent identity formation and role taking skill. In H. D. Grotevant & C. R. Cooper (Eds.), *Adolescent development in the family* (pp. 43-59). San Francisco: Jossey-Bass.

Cox, M. J., Owen, M. T., Henderson, V. K., & Margand, N. (1992). Prediction of infant-father and infant-mother attachment. *Developmental Psychology, 28,* 474-483.

Craik, K. (1943). *The nature of explanation.* Cambridge, UK: Cambridge University Press.

Crittenden, P. M. (1988). Relationships as risk. In J. Belsky & T. Nezworski (Eds.), *Clinical implications of attachment* (pp. 136-174). Hillsdale, NJ: Lawrence Erlbaum.

Crittenden, P. M. (1990). Internal representational models of attachment relationships. *Infant Mental Health Journal, 11,* 259-276.

Crittenden, P. M., Partridge, M. F., & Claussen, A. H. (1992). Family patterns of relationship in normative and dysfunctional families. *Development and Psychopathology, 3,* 491-512.

Crockenberg, S. B. (1981). Infant irritability, mother responsiveness, and social support influences on the security of mother-infant attachment. *Child Development, 52,* 857-865.

Cummings, E. M. (1987). Coping with background anger. *Child Development, 58,* 976-984.

Damon, W. (1977). *The social world of the child.* San Francisco: Jossey-Bass.

Damon, W., & Phelps, E. (1989). Strategic use of peer learning in children's education. In T. J. Berndt & G. W. Ladd (Eds.), *Peer relationships in child development* (pp. 135-157). New York: John Wiley.

Daniels, D., Dunn, J., Furstenberg, E., & Plomin, R. (1985). Environmental differences within the family and adjustment differences within pairs of adolescent siblings. *Child Development, 56,* 764-774.

de Brock, A. J. L., & Vermulst, A. A. (1991, April). *Marital discord, parenting, and child dysfunctioning.* Paper presented at biennial meeting of the Society for Research in Child Development, Seattle, WA.

Denham, S. A. (1986). Social cognition, prosocial behavior, and emotion in preschoolers: Contextual validation. *Child Development, 57,* 194-201.

Dishion, T. J. (1990). The peer context of troublesome child and adolescent behavior. In P. E. Leone (Ed.), *Understanding troubled and troubling youth* (pp. 128-153). Newbury Park, CA: Sage.

Dishion, T. J., Patterson, G. R., Stoolmiller, M., & Skinner, M. L. (1990). *An ecological analysis of boys' drift to antisocial peers: From middle childhood to adolescence.* Oregon Learning Center Paper No. 88-295.

Doise, W., & Mugny, G. (1984). *The social development of the intellect.* Elmsford, NY: Pergamon.

Duck, S. (1989). Socially competent communication and relationship development. In B. H. Schneider, G. Attili, & J. Nadel (Eds.), *Social competence in developmental perspective* (pp. 91-106). Dordrecht, Netherlands: Kluwer.

Dunn, J. (1983). Sibling relationships in early childhood. *Child Development, 54,* 787-811.

Dunn, J. (1988a). *The beginnings of social understanding.* Cambridge, MA: Harvard University Press.

Dunn, J. (1988b). Relations among relationships. In S. Duck (Ed.), *Handbook of personal relationships* (pp. 193-209). New York: John Wiley.

Dunn, J. (in press). Understanding others and the social world: Current issues in developmental research, and their relation to preschool experiences and practice. *Journal of Applied Developmental Research.*

Dunn, J., & Beardsall, L. (in preparation). *Siblings' stories.*

Dunn, J., & Brown, J. (1991). Becoming American or English? Talking about the social world in England and the U.S. In M. Bornstein (Ed.), *Cross cultural approaches to parenting* (pp. 155-172). Hillsdale, NJ: Lawrence Erlbaum.

Dunn, J., & Brown, J. (in press). Early conversations about causality: Content, pragmatics, and developmental change. *British Journal of Developmental Psychology.*

Dunn, J., Brown, J., & Beardsall, L. (1991). Family talk about feeling states and children's later understanding of others' emotions. *Developmental Psychology, 27,* 448-455.

Dunn, J., Brown, J., Slomkowski, C., Tesla, C., & Youngblade, L. (1991). Young children's understanding of other people's feelings and beliefs: Individual differences and their antecedents. *Child Development, 62,* 1352-1366.

Dunn, J., & Dale, N. (1984). I a daddy: Two-year-olds' collaboration in joint pretend play with sibling and with mother. In I. Bretherton (Ed.), *Symbolic play: The development of social understanding* (pp. 131-158). New York: Academic Press.

Dunn, J., & Kendrick, C. (1982). *Siblings: Love, envy, and understanding.* Cambridge, MA: Harvard University Press.

Dunn, J., & McGuire, S. (1992). Sibling and peer relationships in childhood. *Journal of Child Psychology and Psychiatry, 33,* 67-105.

Dunn, J., & Munn, P. (1985). Becoming a family member: Family conflict and the development of social understanding in the second year. *Child Development, 56,* 764-774.

Dunn, J., & Munn, P. (1986). Siblings and prosocial development. *International Journal of Behavioral Development, 9,* 265-284.

Dunn, J., & Munn, P. (1987). The development of justification in disputes. *Developmental Psychology, 23,* 791-798.

Dunn, J., & Plomin, R. (1986). Determinants of maternal behavior towards 3-year-old siblings. *British Journal of Developmental Psychology, 4,* 127-137.

Dunn, J., & Plomin, R. (1990). *Separate lives: Why siblings are so different.* New York: Basic Books.

Dunn, J., Plomin, R., & Daniels, D. (1986). Consistency and change in mothers' behavior towards two-year-old siblings. *Child Development, 57,* 348-356.

Dunn, J., Plomin, R., & Nettles, M. (1985). Consistency of mothers' behavior towards infant siblings. *Developmental Psychology, 21,* 1188-1195.

East, P. L. (1989, April). *Missing provisions in peer-withdrawn and aggressive children's friendships: Do siblings compete?* Paper presented at the biennial meeting of the Society for Research in Child Development, Kansas City, MO.

Easterbrooks, M. A., & Emde, R. N. (1988). Marital and parent-child relationships: The role of affect in the family system. In R. A. Hinde & J. Stevenson-Hinde (Eds.), *Relationships within families: Mutual influences* (pp. 83-103). Oxford, UK: Clarendon.

Eisenberg, N., & Hand, M. (1979). The relationship of preschoolers' reasoning about prosocial moral conflicts to prosocial behavior. *Child Development, 50,* 356-363.

Elder, G. H. (1979). Historical change in life patterns and personality. In P. H. Baltes & O. G. Brim (Eds.), *Lifespan developments and behavior* (Vol. 2, pp. 117-159). New York: John Wiley.

Engfer, A. (1988). The interrelatedness of marriage and the mother-child relationship. In R. A. Hinde & J. Stevenson-Hinde (Eds.), *Relationships within families: Mutual influences* (pp. 104-118). Oxford, UK: Clarendon.

Erikson, E. (1950). *Childhood and society.* New York: Norton.

Fagot, B. I., & Kavanagh, K. (1990). The prediction of antisocial behavior from avoidant attachment classifications. *Child Development, 61,* 864-873.

Field, T. (1984). Separation stress of young children transferring to new schools. *Developmental Psychology, 20,* 786-792.

Fine, G. A. (1980). The natural history of preadolescent male friendship groups. In H. C. Foot, J. Chapman, & J. R. Smith (Eds.), *Friendship and social relations in children* (pp. 293-320). New York: John Wiley.

Floyd, F. J., & Zmich, D. E. (1991). Marriage and the parenting partnership: Perceptions and interactions of parents with mentally retarded and typically developing children. *Child Development, 62,* 1434-1448.

Foot, H. C., Morgan, M. J., & Shute, R. H. (1990). Children's helping relations: An overview. In H. C. Foot, M. J. Morgan, & R. H. Shute (Eds.), *Children helping children* (pp. 3-17). New York: John Wiley.

Fox, N. A. (1989). The psychophysiological correlates of emotional reactivity during the first year of life. *Developmental Psychology, 25,* 364-372.

Fox, N. A., Kimmerly, N. L., & Schafer, W. D. (1991). Attachment to mother/attachment to father: A meta-analysis. *Child Development, 62,* 210-225.

Freud, S. (1949). *An outline of psychoanalysis.* New York: Norton.

Frodi, A. M., Lamb, M. E., Frodi, M., Hwang, C., Forrstrom, B., & Corry, T. (1982). Stability and change in parental attitudes following an infant's birth into traditional and nontraditional Swedish families. *Scandinavian Journal of Psychology, 23,* 53-62.

Frye, D., & Moore, C. (1991). *Children's theories of mind: Mental states and social understanding.* Hillsdale, NJ: Lawrence Erlbaum.

Furman, W., & Buhrmester, D. (1985). Children's perceptions of the personal relationships in their social networks. *Developmental Psychology, 21,* 1016-1024.

Gable, S., Belsky, J., & Crnic, K. (in press). Marriage, parenting, and child development: Progress and prospects. *Journal of Family Psychology.*

Garber, J., & Dodge, K. (1991). *The development of affect and dysregulation.* Cambridge, UK: Cambridge University Press.

Garvey, C. (1977). *Play.* Cambridge, MA: Harvard University Press.

Garvey, C. (1984). *Children's talk.* London: Fontana.

Gershman, E. S., & Hayes, D. S. (1983). Differential stability of reciprocal friendships and unilateral friendships among preschool children. *Merrill-Palmer Quarterly, 29,* 169-177.

Goldberg, W. A., & Easterbrooks, M. A. (1984). Role of marital quality in toddler development. *Developmental Psychology, 20,* 504-514.

Goldsmith, H. H., & Alansky, J. A. (1987). Maternal and infant temperamental predictors of attachment: A meta-analytic review. *Journal of Consulting and Clinical Psychology, 55,* 805-816.

Goldsmith, H. H., Bradshaw, D. L., & Rieser-Danner, L. A. (1986). Temperament as a potential developmental influence on attachment. In J. V. Lerner & R. M. Lerner (Eds.), *Temperament and social interaction during infancy and childhood* (pp. 5-34). San Francisco: Jossey-Bass.

Goodyer, I. M., Wright, C., & Altham, P. M. E. (1989). Recent friendships in anxious and depressed school age children. *Psychological Medicine, 19,* 165-174.

Goth-Owens, T. L., Stollak, G. A., Messe, L. A., Peshkess, I., & Watts, P. (1982). Marital satisfaction, parenting satisfaction, and parenting behavior in early infancy. *Infant Mental Health Journal, 3,* 187-197.

Gottlieb, L. N., & Mendelson, M. J. (1990). Parental support and firstborn girls' adaptation to the birth of a sibling. *Journal of Applied Developmental Psychology, 11,* 29-48.

Gottman, J. M. (1986). The observation of social process. In J. M. Gottman & J. G. Parker (Eds.), *Conversations of friends: Speculations on affective development* (pp. 51-100). Cambridge, UK: Cambridge University Press.

Gottman, J. M., & Mettetal, G. (1986). Speculations about social and affective development: Friendship and acquaintanceship through adolescence. In J. M. Gottman & J. G. Parker (Eds.), *Conversations of friends: Speculations on affective development* (pp. 192-237). Cambridge, UK: Cambridge University Press.

Gottman, J. M., & Parker, J. G. (Eds.) (1986). *Conversations of friends: Speculations on affective development.* Cambridge, UK: Cambridge University Press.

Grossmann, K., Fremmer-Bombik, E., Rudolph, J., & Grossmann, K. E. (1988). Maternal attachment representations as related to patterns of infant-mother attachment and maternal care during the first year. In R. A. Hinde & J. Stevenson-Hinde (Eds.), *Relationships within families: Mutual influences* (pp. 241-260). Oxford, UK: Clarendon.

Grossmann, K., & Grossmann, K. E. (1991). Attachment quality as an organizer of emotional and behavioral responses in longitudinal perspective. In C. M. Parkes, J. Stevenson-Hinde, & P. Morris (Eds.), *Attachment across the life cycle* (pp. 93-114). London: Tavistock/Routledge.

Harris, K. M., & Morgan, S. P. (1991). Fathers, sons, and daughters: Differential paternal involvement in parenting. *Journal of Marriage and the Family, 53,* 531-544.

Harter, S. (1983). Developmental perspectives on the self system. In E. M. Hetherington (Ed.), *Handbook of child psychology: Social and personality development* (pp. 275-385). New York: John Wiley.

Hartup, W. W. (1983). Peer relations. In P. H. Mussen (Ed.), *Handbook of child psychology: Vol. 4. Socialization, personality, and social development* (pp. 103-196). New York: John Wiley.

Hartup, W. W. (1986). On relationships and development. In W. W. Hartup & Z. Rubin (Eds.), *Relationships and development* (pp. 1-26). Hillsdale, NJ: Lawrence Erlbaum.

Hartup, W. W. (1989). Behavioral manifestations of children's friendships. In T. J. Berndt & G. W. Ladd (Eds.), *Peer relationships in child development* (pp. 46-70). New York: John Wiley.

Hartup, W. W., Laursen, B., Stewart, M. I., & Eastenson, A. (1988). Conflict and the friendship relations of young children. *Child Development, 59*, 1590-1600.

Hayes, C. D., Palmer, J. L., & Zaslow, M. J. (1990). *Who cares for America's children?* Washington, DC: National Academy Press.

Hetherington, E. M. (1988). Parents, children, and siblings: Six years after divorce. In R. A. Hinde & J. Stevenson-Hinde (Eds.), *Relationships within families: Mutual influences* (pp. 311-331). Oxford, UK: Oxford University Press.

Hinde, R. A. (1979). *Towards understanding relationships.* London: Academic Press.

Hinde, R. A. (1982). Attachment: Some conceptual and biological issues. In C. M. Parkes & J. Stevenson-Hinde (Eds.), *The place of attachment in human behavior* (pp. 60-76). London: Tavistock.

Hinde, R. A. (1987). *Individuals, relationships and culture.* Cambridge, UK: Cambridge University Press.

Hinde, R. A. (1988). Continuities and discontinuities: Conceptual issues and methodological considerations. In M. Rutter (Ed.), *Studies of psychosocial risk* (pp. 367-383). Cambridge, UK: Cambridge University Press.

Hinde, R. A. (1990). Commentary. *Human Development, 33*, 283-288.

Hinde, R. A. (1992). Developmental psychology in the context of other behavioral sciences. *Developmental Psychology, 28*, 1018-1029.

Hinde, R. A., & Stevenson-Hinde, J. (1988). Epilogue. In R. A. Hinde & J. Stevenson-Hinde (Eds.), *Relationships within families: Mutual influences* (pp. 365-385). Oxford, UK: Clarendon.

Hinde, R. A., Tamplin, A., & Barrett, J. (In press, a). Individual characteristics, child-mother and child-younger sibling interactions of 4-year-olds. *Early Development and Parenting.*

Hinde, R. A., Tamplin, A., & Barrett, J. (In press, b). Consistency within and between relationships. *Man and Society.*

Hinde, R. A., & Tobin, C. (1986). Temperament at home and behaviour at preschool. In G. A. Kohnstamm (Ed.). *Temperament discussed* (pp. 123-132). Lisse, Netherlands: Swets & Zeitlinger.

Hobart, C. J. (1987, April). *Behavioral interactions of friends and acquaintances in childhood and adolescence.* Paper presented at biennial meeting of the Society for Research in Child Development, Baltimore, MD.

Hodges, J., & Tizard, B. (1989). Social and family relationships of ex-institutional adolescents. *Journal of Child Psychology and Psychiatry, 30*, 77-98.

Howe, N., & Ross, H. S. (1990). Socialization perspective-taking, and the sibling relationship. *Developmental Psychology, 26*, 160-165.

Howes, C. (1987). Peer interaction of young children. *Monographs of the Society for Research in Child Development* (Serial Number 217, Vol. 53, No. 1).

Howes, C., Unger, O., & Matheson, C. (1992). *The collaborative construction of pretend.* Albany: State University of New York Press.

Kagan, J. (1982). *Psychological research on the human infant: An evaluative summary.* New York: W. T. Grant.

Kaufman, J., & Zigler, E. (1986). *Do abused children become abusive parents?* Unpublished manuscript, Yale University, New Haven, CT.

Kaye, K., & Furstenberg, F. F. (Eds.). (1985). *Child Development, 56,* 279-501.

Kendrick, C., & Dunn, J. (1982). Protest or pleasure? The response of firstborn children to interactions between their mothers and infant siblings. *Journal of Child Psychology and Psychiatry, 23,* 117-129.

Kendrick, C., & Dunn, J. (1983). Sibling quarrels and maternal responses. *Developmental Psychology, 19,* 62-71.

Kenny, D. A., & La Voie, L. (1984). The social relations model. In L. Berkowitz (Ed.), *Advances in experimental social psychology* (Vol. 19, pp. 141-182). New York: Academic Press.

Koch, H. L. (1960). The relation of certain formal attributes of siblings to attitudes held toward each other and toward their parents. *Monographs of the Society for Research in Child Development,* Vol. 25, No. 4.

Kramer, L. (1990). Becoming a sibling: With a little help from my friends. In M. Mendelson (Chair), *Becoming a sibling: Adjustment, roles, and relationships.* Symposium at the 7th International Conference on Infant Studies, Montreal.

Kreppner, K., & Lerner, R. M. (1989). *Family systems and life-span development.* Hillsdale, NJ: Lawrence Erlbaum.

Lamb, M. E., Thompson, R. A., Gardner, W., & Charnov, E. L. (1985). *Infant-mother attachment.* Hillsdale, NJ: Lawrence Erlbaum.

Lewis, M., & Feiring, C. (1989). Early predictors of childhood friendship. In T. J. Berndt & G. W. Ladd (Eds.), *Peer relationships in child development* (pp. 246-273). New York: John Wiley.

Maccoby, E. E. (1990). Gender and relationships. *American Psychologist, 45,* 513-520.

Maccoby, E. E., & Martin, J. A. (1983). Socialization in the context of the family: Parent-child interaction. In P. H. Mussen (Ed.), *Handbook of child psychology: Vol. 4. Socialization, personality, and social development* (pp. 1-101). New York: John Wiley.

MacDonald, K., & Parke, R. (1984). Bridging the gap: Parent-child play interaction and peer interactive competence. *Child Development, 55,* 1265-1277.

Mahler, M. S., Pine, F., & Bergman, A. (1975). *The psychological birth of the infant.* New York: Basic Books.

Main, M., Kaplan, N., & Cassidy, J. (1985). Security in infancy, childhood, and adolescence: A move to the level of representation. In I. Bretherton & E. Waters (Eds.), *Growing points in attachment theory and research. Monographs of the Society for Research in Child Development, 50* (1-2, Serial No. 209).

Masten, A. S., Garmezy, N., Tellegen, A., Pellegrini, D. S., Larkin, K., & Larsen, A. (1968). Competence and stress in school children: The moderating effects of individual and family qualities. *Journal of Clinical Child Psychology and Psychiatry, 29,* 745-764.

Matsumoto, D., Haan, N., Yabrove, G., Theodorou, P., & Carney, C. C. (1986). Preschoolers' moral actions and emotions in Prisoners' Dilemma. *Developmental Psychology, 22,* 663-670.

McCartney, K. (1990). *Child care and maternal employment: A social ecology approach.* San Francisco: Jossey-Bass.

McGhee, S. A. (1989). *Humor and social interaction: A study of children's use and appreciation of humor in everyday situations.* Unpublished master's thesis, Pennsylvania State University, University Park, PA.

McHale, S. M., Crouter, A. C., & Bartko, W. T. (in press). Traditional and egalitarian patterns of parental involvement: Antecedents, consequences, and temporal rhythms. In D. Featherman, R. Lerner, & M. Perlmutter (Eds.), *Lifespan development and behavior* (Vol. 2,   ). Hillsdale, NJ: Lawrence Erlbaum.

McHale, S. M., Freitag, M. K., Crouter, A. C., & Bartko, W. T. (1991). Connections between dimensions of marital quality and school-aged children's adjustment. *Journal of Applied Developmental Psychology, 12,* 1-17.

Mendelson, M. J., & Aboud, F. E. (1991, April). *Kindergartners' personality, popularity, and friendships.* Poster presented at biennial meeting of the Society for Research in Child Development, Seattle, Washington.

Meyer, H-J. (1988). Marital and mother-child relationships: Developmental history, parent personality, and child difficultness. In R. A. Hinde & J. Stevenson-Hinde (Eds.), *Relationships within families: Mutual influences* (pp. 119-139). Oxford, UK: Clarendon.

Miell, D. E., & Duck, S. (1986). Strategies in developing friendship. In V. J. Derlega & B. A. Winstead (Eds.), *Friendship and social interaction* (pp. 129-144). New York: Springer-Verlag.

Minuchin, P. (1985). Families and individual development: Provocations from the field of family therapy. *Child Development, 56,* 289-302.

Morris, D. (1980). *Infant attachment and problem solving in the toddler: Relations to mother's family history.* Unpublished doctoral dissertation, University of Minnesota, Minneapolis, MN.

Morris, D. (1981). Attachment and intimacy. In G. Stricker (Ed.), *Intimacy* (pp. 305-323). New York: Plenum.

Munn, P. (1989). *The development of understanding of social rules between the ages of 24 and 36 months.* Unpublished doctoral dissertation, Cambridge University, UK.

Munn, P., & Dunn, J. (1989). Temperament and the developing relationship between young siblings. *International Journal of Behavioral Development, 12,* 433-451.

Nelson, J., & Aboud, F. E. (1985). The resolution of social conflict between friends. *Child Development, 56,* 1009-1017.

Newson, J., & Newson, E. (1970). *Four years old in an urban community.* London: Penguin.

Park, K. A., Lay, K., & Ramsay, L. (1990, March). *Stability and change in preschoolers' friendships.* Paper presented at the Conference on Human Development, Richmond, VA.

Park, K. A., & Waters, E. (1989). Security of attachment and preschool friendships. *Child Development, 60,* 1076-1081.

Parke, R. D. (1978). Parent-infant interaction: Progress, paradigms, problems. In G. P. Sackett (Ed.), *Observing behavior* (Vol. 1, pp. 69-94). Baltimore: University Park Press.

Parke, R. D., & Ladd, G. W. (Eds.). (1992). *Family-peer relationships: Modes of linkage.* Hillsdale, NJ: Lawrence Erlbaum.

Parke, R. D., MacDonald, K., Beitel, A., & Bhavnagri, N. (1988). The role of the family in the development of peer relationships. In K. Kreppner & R. M.

Lerner (Eds.), *Family systems and life span development* (pp. 65-92). Hillsdale, NJ: Lawrence Erlbaum.

Parke, R. D., & Sawin, D. B. (1980). The family in early infancy: Social interactional and attitudinal analyses. In F. A. Pedersen (Ed.), *The father-infant relationship* (pp. 44-70). New York: Praeger.

Parker, J. G. (1986). Becoming friends: Conversational skills for friendship formation in young children. In J. M. Gottman & J. G. Parker (Eds.), *Conversations of friends: Speculations on affective development* (pp. 103-138). Cambridge, UK: Cambridge University Press.

Parker, J. G., & Asher, S. R. (1987). Peer relations and later personal adjustment: Are low-accepted children at risk? *Psychological Bulletin, 102,* 357-389.

Parker, J. G., & Asher, S. R. (1990, April). *Friendship adjustment, group acceptance, and feelings of loneliness and social dissatisfaction in childhood.* Paper presented at annual meeting of the American Educational Research Association, Boston.

Parker, J. G., & Gottman, J. M. (1989). Social and emotional development in a relational context: Friendship interaction from early childhood to adolescence. In T. J. Berndt & G. W. Ladd (Eds.), *Peer relationships in child development* (pp. 95-131). New York: John Wiley.

Parsons, T., & Bales, R. F. (1956). *Family socialization and interaction process.* London: Routledge & Kegan Paul.

Patterson, G. R. (1984). Siblings: Fellow travellers in coercive family processes. *Advances in the Study of Aggression, 1,* 173-214.

Patterson, G. R. (1986). The contribution of siblings to training for fighting: A microsocial analysis. In D. Olweus, J. Block, & M. Radke-Yarrow (Eds.), *Development of antisocial and prosocial behavior: Research, theories, and issues* (pp. 235-261). New York: Academic Press.

Patterson, G. R., Vaden, N. A., & Kupersmidt, J. B. (in press). Family background, recent life events, and peer rejection during childhood. *Journal of Social and Personal Psychology.*

Perner, J., Ruffman, T., & Leekham, S. R. (submitted). *Theory of mind is contagious: You catch it from your sibs.*

Pettit, G. S., Harrist, A. W., Bates, J. E., & Dodge, K. A. (in press). Family interaction, social cognition, and children's subsequent relations with peers at kindergarten. *Journal of Social and Personal Relationships.*

Piaget, J. (1965). *The moral judgment of the child.* New York: Academic Press.

Pierrehumbert, B., Ianotti, R. J., Cummings, E. M., & Zahn-Waxler, C. (1989). Social functioning with mother and peers at 2 and 5 years: The influence of attachment. *International Journal of Behavioral Development, 12,* 85-100.

Plomin, R., & Bergeman, C. S. (1991). The nature of nurture: Genetic influence on "environmental" measures. *Behavioral and Brain Sciences, 14,* 373-427.

Plomin, R., & Daniels, D. (1987). Why are children in the same family so different from one another? *Behavioral and Brain Sciences, 10,* 1-16.

Plomin, R., & Neiderhiser, J. M. (1992). Genetics and experience. *Current Directions in Psychological Science, 1,* 160-163.

Putallaz, M. (1987). Maternal behavior and children's sociometric status. *Child Development, 54,* 1417-1426.

Putallaz, M., & Heflin, A. H. (1990). Parent-child interaction. In S. R. Asher & J. D. Coie (Eds.), *Peer rejection in childhood* (pp. 189-216). Cambridge, UK: Cambridge University Press.

Quinton, D., & Rutter, M. (1988). *Parenting breakdown: The making and breaking of intergenerational links.* London: Avebury.

Radke-Yarrow, M., Richters, J., & Wilson, W. E. (1988). Child development in a network of relationships. In R. A Hinde & J. Stevenson-Hinde (Eds.), *Relationships within families* (pp. 48-67). Oxford, UK: Clarendon.

Radke-Yarrow, M., Zahn-Waxler, C., & Chapman, M. (1983). Children's prosocial dispositions and behavior. In P. H. Mussen (Ed.), *Handbook of child psychology: Vol. 4. Socialization, personality, and social development* (pp. 469-545). New York: John Wiley.

Raffaelli, M. (1991, April). *Interpersonal conflict with siblings and friends: Implications for early adolescent development.* Paper presented at biennial meeting of the Society for Research in Child Development, Seattle, WA.

Ricks, M. H. (1985). The social transmission of parental behavior: Attachment across generations. In I. Bretherton & E. Waters (Eds.), *Growing points of attachment* (pp. 211-227). *Monographs of the Society for Research in Adolescence, 50* (1-2, Serial No. 209).

Rogoff, B. (1990). *Apprenticeship in thinking: Cognitive development in social context.* Oxford, UK: Oxford University Press.

Roopnarine, J. L., & Honig, A. S. (1985, September). The unpopular child. *Young Children,* pp. 59-65.

Ross, H. S., & Lollis, S. P. (1989). A social relations analysis of toddler peer relationships. *Child Development, 60,* 1082-1091.

Rowe, D. C. (1989). Families and peers. In T. J. Berndt & G. W. Ladd (Eds.), *Peer relationships in child development* (pp. 274-299). New York: John Wiley.

Rubin, K. H., Bream, L. A., & Rose-Krasnor, L. (in press). Social problem solving and aggression in childhood. In D. Pepler & K. H. Rubin (Eds.), *The development and treatment of childhood aggression.* Hillsdale, NJ: Lawrence Erlbaum.

Rutter, M. (1988). Functions and consequences of relationships: Some psychopathological considerations. In R. A. Hinde & J. Stevenson-Hinde (Eds.), *Relationships within families: Mutual influences* (pp. 332-353). Oxford, UK: Clarendon.

Rutter, M. (1991). A fresh look at maternal deprivation. In P. Bateson (Ed.), *The development and integration of behaviour: Essays in honour of Robert Hinde* (pp. 331-374). Cambridge, UK: Cambridge University Press.

Scarr, S., & Grajek, S. (1982). Similarities and differences among siblings. In M. E. Lamb & B. Sutton-Smith (Eds.), *Sibling relationships: Their nature and significance across the lifespan* (pp. 357-381). Hillsdale, NJ: Lawrence Erlbaum.

Selman, R. (1980). *The growth of interpersonal understanding: Developmental and clinical analyses.* New York: Academic Press.

Sigman, M., & Ungerer, J. (1984). Attachment behaviors in autistic children. *Journal of Autism and Developmental Disorders, 14,* 231-244.

Slomkowski, C. M., & Dunn, J. (1992). Arguments and relationships within the family: Differences in children's disputes with mother and sibling. *Developmental Psychology, 28,* 919-924.

Slomkowski, C. M., & Dunn, J. (submitted, a). *How children connect: The nature and correlates of early sibling and friend relationships.*

Slomkowski, C. M., & Dunn, J. (submitted, b). *Young children's views of moral transgressions with friends and siblings.*

Slomkowski, C. M., & Killen, M. (in press). Young children's conceptions of transgressions with friends and nonfriends. *International Journal of Behavioral Development.*

Sroufe, L. A. (1983). Infant-caregiver attachment and patterns of adaptation in the preschool: The roots of competence and maladaptation. In R. N. Emde & R. J. Harmon (Eds.), *The development of attachment and affiliative systems* (pp. 281-292). New York: Plenum.

Sroufe, L. A., Egeland, B., & Kreutzer, T. (1990). The fate of early experience following developmental change: Longitudinal approaches to individual adaptation in childhood. *Child Development, 61,* 1363-1373.

Sroufe, L. A., & Fleeson, J. (1986). Attachment and the construction of relationships. In W. Hartup & Z. Rubin (Eds.), *Relationships and development.* Hillsdale, NJ: Lawrence Erlbaum.

Sroufe, L. A., & Waters, E. (1977). Attachment as an organizational construct. *Child Development, 48,* 1184-1199.

Sroufe, L. A., & Wunsch, J. (1972). The development of laughter in the first year of life. *Child Development, 43,* 1326-1344.

Stevenson-Hinde, J., Hinde, R. A., & Simpson, A. E. (1986). Behavior at home and friendly or hostile behavior in preschool. In D. Olweus, J. Block, & M. Radke-Yarrow (Eds.), *Development of antisocial and prosocial behavior* (pp. 127-145). New York: Academic Press.

Stevenson-Hinde, J., & Shouldice, A. (1990). Fear and attachment in 2.5-year-olds. *British Journal of Developmental Psychology, 8,* 319-333.

Stewart, R. B., & Marvin, R. S. (1984). Sibling relations: The role of conceptual perspective-taking in the ontogeny of sibling caregiving. *Child Development, 55,* 1322-1332.

Stewart, R. B., Mobley, L. A., Van Tuyl, S. S., & Salvador, M. A. (1987). The firstborn's adjustment to the birth of a sibling. Child Development, 58, 341-355.

Stifter, C. A., & Fox, N. A. (1990). Infant reactivity: Physiological correlates of newborn and five-month temperament. *Developmental Psychology, 26,* 582-588.

Stocker, C., & Dunn, J. (1990). Sibling relationships in childhood: Links with friendships and peer relationships. *The British Journal of Developmental Psychology, 8,* 227-244.

Stocker, C., Dunn, J., & Plomin, R. (1989). Sibling relationships: Links with child temperament, maternal behavior, and family structure. *Child Development, 60,* 715-727.

Stocker, C. M., & Mantz-Simmons, L. M. (in press). *Children's friendships and peer status: Links with family relationships, temperament and social skills.*

Stoneman, Z., Brody, G. H., & Burke, M. (1989). Marital quality, depression, and inconsistent parenting: Relationship with observed mother-child conflict. *American Journal of Orthopsychiatry, 59,* 105-117.

Stoneman, Z., Brody, G. H., & McKinnon, C. E. (1984). Naturalistic observations of children's roles and activities while playing with their siblings and friends. *Child Development, 55,* 617-627.

Sullivan, H. S. (1953). *The interpersonal theory of psychiatry.* New York: Norton.

Tesla, C., & Dunn, J. (1992). Getting along or getting your way: The development of young children's argument in conflicts with mother and sibling. *Social Development, 1,* 107-121.

Teti, D. M., & Ablard, K. E. (1989). Security of attachment and infant-sibling relationships: A laboratory study. *Child Development, 60,* 1519-1528.

Teti, D. M., Bond, L. A., & Gibbs, E. D. (1986). Sibling-created experiences: Relationships to birth-spacing and infant cognitive development. *Infant Behavior and Development, 9,* 27-42.

Teti, D. M., Bond, L. A., & Gibbs, E. D. (1989). Sibling interaction, birth spacing, and intellectual/linguistic development. In P. Zukow (Ed.), *Sibling relationships across cultures* (pp. 117-139). New York: Springer-Verlag.

Thompson, R. A., Connell, J. P., & Bridges, L. J. (1988). Temperament, emotion, and social interactive behavior in the Strange Situation: An analysis of attachment system functioning. *Child Development, 59,* 1102-1110.

Vandell, D. L. (1987). Baby sister/baby brother: Reactions to the birth of a sibling and patterns of early sibling relations. *Journal of Children in Contemporary Society, 19,* 13-37.

Vandell, D. L., Minnet, A. M., Johnson, B. S., & Santrock, J. W. (1990). *Siblings and friends: Experiences of school-aged children.* Unpublished manuscript, University of Texas at Dallas.

Van Ijzendoorn, M. H., & Kroonenberg, P. H. (1988). Cross-cultural patterns of attachment: A meta-analysis of the Strange Situation. *Child Development, 59,* 147-156.

Vaughn, B. E., Egeland, B., Sroufe, L. A., & Waters, E. (1979). Individual differences in infant-mother attachment at twelve and eighteen months: Stability and change in families under stress. *Child Development, 50,* 971-975.

Vaughn, B. E., Lefever, G. B., Seifer, R., & Barglow, P. (1989). Attachment behavior, attachment security, and temperament during infancy. *Child Development, 60,* 728-737.

Vaughn, B. E., Stevenson-Hinde, J., Waters, E., Kotsaftis, A., Lefever, G. B., Shouldice, A., Trudel, M., & Belsky, J. (1992). Attachment security and temperament in infancy and early childhood: Some conceptual clarifications. *Developmental Psychology, 28,* 463-473.

Vygotsky, L. S. (1978). *Mind in society: The development of higher psychological processes.* Cambridge, MA: Harvard University Press.

Ward, M. J., Vaughn, B. E., & Robb, M. D. (1988). Social-emotional adaptation and infant-mother attachment in siblings: Role of the mother in cross-sibling consistency. *Child Development, 59,* 643-651.

Weissman, S., & Cohen, R. S. (1985). The parenting alliance and adolescence. *Adolescent Psychiatry, 12,* 24-45.

Wellman, H. M. (1990). *The child's theory of mind.* Cambridge: MIT Press.

Whiten, A. (1991). *Natural theories of mind.* Oxford, UK: Blackwell.

Youngblade, L. M., & Belsky, J. (1992). Parent-child antecedents of five-year-olds' close friendships: A longitudinal analysis. *Developmental Psychology, 1,* 107-121.

Youngblade, L. M., & Dunn, J. (submitted). *Individual differences in young children's pretend play with mother and sibling: Links to relationship quality and understanding of other people's feelings and beliefs.*

Youngblade, L. M., Park, K. A., & Belsky, J. (submitted). *Measurement of young children's close friendship: A comparison of two independent assessment systems and their association with attachment security.*

Zahn-Waxler, C., Denham, S., Ianotti, R. J., & Cummings, E. M. (1991). Peer relations in children with a depressed caregiver. In R. D. Parke & G. W. Ladd (Eds.), *Family-peer relationships: Modes of linkage* (pp. 317-344). Hillsdale, NJ: Lawrence Erlbaum.

Zahn-Waxler, C., & Radke-Yarrow, M. (1982). The development of altruism: Alternative research strategies. In N. Eisenberg-Berg (Ed.), *The development of prosocial behavior* (pp. 109-137). New York: Academic Press.

Zukow, P. G. (1989). *Sibling interaction across cultures.* New York: Springer-Verlag.

Index

About the Author

Judy Dunn is Distinguished Professor of Human Development at The Pennsylvania State University. Before coming to the United States she carried out research at the Medical Research Council Unit on the Development and Integration of Behaviour at the University of Cambridge, where she was a Fellow of King's College. Her interests center on the development of children's relationships and social understanding; she pioneered research on children's sibling relationships and the use of naturalistic observations to study social understanding, and has conducted longitudinal studies of children in both the United States and the United Kingdom. Her previous books include *Siblings* (1982), *The Beginnings of Social Understanding* (1988), and with Robert Plomin, *Separate Lives* (1990).

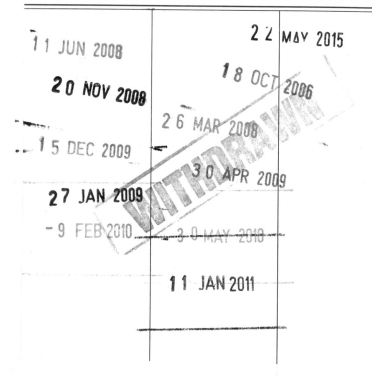
Printed in the United Kingdom
by Lightning Source UK Ltd.
110090UKS00001B/43-51

9 780803 944916